LIFE *of* MAMILS

My Life as a Middle Aged Man in Lycra

Martin Gatenby

Fisher King Publishing

Copyright © 2016 Martin Gatenby

Life of Mamils

Fisher King Publishing Ltd, The Studio, Arthington Lane

Pool in Wharfedale, LS21 1JZ, England

www.fisherkingpublishing.co.uk

Cover design: Martin Procter

A CIP catalogue record of this book is available from
the British Library

ISBN 978-1-910406-48-9

Dedication

To Ned, Louis, Guy and Lesley, for all the times I have left you sleeping.

To mum and dad, for the lifts and shouts of encouragement from the roadside (sorry about the swearing mum - I only wanted to tell the truth).

To the much missed Willie Tyler – a legend of a man who bought me a Puch Pathfinder instead of a Raleigh Chopper.

And to anyone, anywhere, who has ever struggled to ride a bike uphill, fuelled by nothing other than a desire to get to the top. Chapeau!

Acknowledgements

The first charity ride that Dicco and I did was on behalf of Brain Tumour Research and Support across Yorkshire (BTRS). We still do the ride each year in May. It is now based on a circular route starting and finishing in Wetherby, West Yorkshire. Details can be found on the charity's web site www.BTRS.org.uk

Thank you to Martin Proctor at MPD Associates for the cover design – further examples of his work appear regularly in *Rouleur* magazine. He has also been a valued friend and riding partner for many hundreds of miles over recent years.

'DS' James Lovell, founder of the Cappuccino Cycling Club, is both directly and indirectly responsible for many of the events that make up this story, and I would like to thank him, and all the members of the club for their friendship and company as we have shared our cycling journey together. Information about the club can be found on the web site www.cappuccinoclub.co.uk

Much of this story would never have happened without the help of the Rheumatology team at Harrogate District Hospital, in particular Beverley and Esther, the research nurses who gave me so much support. I am eternally thankful to them.

Thank you to Rick Armstrong and the team at Fisher King Publishing for the opportunity to turn my story into a book.

Contents

Prologue

In the early nineteen-seventies, on about the third Saturday each May, families across England would sit down together to watch television. Across the country, roads would be quiet, shops would be empty and Mums, Dads and their children would gather.

In our house, my Auntie Joyce and Uncle Ron would come over to visit with my cousins, Andrew, Ian, Nicholas and Judith. We'd squeeze onto the sofa and the extra chairs that only usually came out at Christmas. The excitement would steadily increase until, at three o'clock, the FA cup final would kick off.

It seems hard to believe that this family ritual was almost as well observed across the country as Christmas Day, but, apart from during the world cup, it was the only time that live football made it onto television screens, and as far as I remember, nearly everyone sat down to watch it, regardless of who was playing.

I recall, as a young boy, seeing the match in colour for the first time and thinking how green the grass at Wembley stadium looked in the May sunshine, and how I'd love to run out onto that very pitch one day.

Every single boy I knew had that very same dream. Every single boy wanted to be only one thing when he grew up – a footballer.

During the 1974 world cup, when my Mum and Dad had bought their first colour television, my brother Neil and I would run into the garden as soon as the game we were watching had finished, and play football. I would be Gerd Muller, and he'd be Johan Cruyff. All our dreams were about football.

On one of those sunny afternoons, we were recovering from

our latest football match and sat gulping orange squash while contemplating going out to play on our bikes. Our Grandad Tyler told us that if we were good from that day until Christmas, he'd buy us both a Raleigh Chopper. We were amazed. With its high handlebars, huge rear wheel and three speed stick shift gears, the Chopper was the ultimate two wheeled symbol of style and desirability. It had even been featured on every child's favourite television program, Blue Peter, when the three presenters had wobbled their way around the studio, whilst one of them described the Chopper as 'the most modern looking bike I've ever seen'. Owning a Chopper guaranteed you a place amongst the coolest of your peers.

Then, later that summer, I saw something on television that changed all my dreams.

I saw men struggling to ride skinny racing bikes up mountains, rocking from side to side, with agony on their faces and pain in their eyes. I saw people running alongside them and screaming encouragement into their ears, whilst the commentator's voice crackled over what sounded like a telephone line as he became more and more excited about what he was seeing. I witnessed something that has stuck with me throughout my life I saw the Tour de France.

That afternoon, I didn't go out and play football. I got on my little bike, called for my friends and we played 'Tour de France', trying to recreate, in our childish imaginations, what I had just seen and heard.

I didn't want a Raleigh Chopper, I didn't want to be a footballer. I wasn't bothered about running out at Wembley...

...My dreams lay elsewhere.

Stage 1
Boyhood Dreams

The sun is just climbing above the rooftops around the square in the Southern French village of Valbonne, and the regulars at the Cafe des Arcades are vying for position around the old television propped on a table. Waiters carrying trays of coffee and steaming bowls of pasta are doing their best not trip over the power lead that runs from the bar across the terrace to the outside tables under the shade of the trees along the top of the square. The summer of July 1999 is just as busy as any other summer, but this year the waiters, busy as they are, have one eye on the television that seems to be the centre of attention for most of their customers.

English tourists ask what the fuss is about, only to be teased that they've never heard of 'our boy'- the English lad who lives up the valley and who sits in this very cafe almost every day in the winter sipping milky coffee and eating pain au raisin, or meeting some of the locals to race up to the observatory at the top of the mountain, before hurtling back down the valley, overtaking cars and coming back to the square to while away the afternoon relaxing in the winter sunshine. The waiters are fed up of explaining what the 'le Tour' is, and why the whole village seems to have come to a standstill during every afternoon this month, and why today could be *the* day. The day their adopted son finds himself on top of the world and all over tomorrow's papers, and why a cycling jersey hangs in a frame behind the bar, and why they're hoping for a new yellow one to hang in its place at the end of summer.

At the same time, a thousand miles North, the bar of The Coach and Horses, the only pub in the UK to advertise 'Live Cycling on the Big Screen', is starting to fill with an excited and chatty bunch of friends who only wish they could have managed more time off work, and that they could be packed into a motor home on the slopes of an alpine mountain in the scorching July sun. Other drinkers wonder what is going on, and why there is so much fuss.

From the village of Bourg d'Oisans, all the way up the snaking mountain road, around each of its twenty-one hairpins, a crowd of almost a quarter of a million people are getting more and more excited, a few nursing hangovers from the night before, many doing their best to finish off the supplies of gradually warming beer. The wildest party is taking place at the seventh corner from the top – 'Dutch Corner' is a sea of orange and the fans dance and sing as they wait for the race to arrive. Elsewhere, people paint names in the road whilst the police look on, directing traffic through the crowd. Occasionally cyclists pick their way through the chaos, encouraged by slaps on the back, and cries of 'Allez, allez'.

Eventually the procession of bizarre vehicles that make up the publicity caravan snakes by, and there's a huge scramble to pick up the useless tit bits thrown to the crowd, from pens advertising supermarkets, to bits of smoked cheese and cardboard hats with garish logos. Loud music blasts from every passing float, and young and beautiful students from Paris dance along, urging everyone to join in, whilst they spend their summer holidays at a three week party of free booze and bed hopping evenings around the whole of France. The anticipation builds and builds.

Finally, here they come. A swarm of out-riding motorcycles, and somewhere in the middle the two cyclists, eyeing each other carefully, taking on as much water as they can from their bottles before throwing them to the roadside where they are pounced upon by people seeking the ultimate tour souvenir. The crowds are going crazy, running into the road and screaming in the riders ears – 'Allez, allez' allez', pouring water onto their sweating heads, giving them the occasional push, then falling by the wayside as the riders go on towards the sky.

Back in the Coach and Horses, television commentator David Duffield's voice is getting louder. He's stopped talking about the crème brulee he enjoyed in last night's hotel and is starting to get carried away. Next to him, his co-commentator, the normally so relaxed and measured Sean Kelly, is also getting excited.

'So Sean what's he going to do; you've ridden this road many times - when's the best place to attack? How's he going to shake off the German? Do you think he can do it? Do you think he looks tired? What's going through his mind? Do you think he'll do it?'

'Ah well you know David, he looks tired and he must know it's going to be hard, its one or the other by the end of today, if Ulrich pulls away then our man's going to lose, but they've both got enough time in hand to take the race today. He just has to time his attack right, Ulrich looks good so we'll have to see what he can do'.

The regulars in the Cafe des Arcade are much more relaxed than Mr. Duffield, but even they are starting to stand up and shout at the television. The village square has come to a standstill and everyone knows it's now or never...

On the mountain Gatenby is really feeling the heat. The sun is high in the sky and the temperature has reached over forty degrees Celsius, even in the scarce areas that are shaded by the spruce trees. Looking down at the square metre of road in front of his wheel, he can feel the sweat pouring off his head and splashing onto his knees. No matter how much he drinks, he still feels thirsty, and the liquid already in his stomach makes him feel like he's been kicked by a horse. He can hear and feel every breath, every heartbeat, even above the screaming spectators. 'Surely Ulrich feels as bad as me, surely he's hurting as well'. He looks across at his rival, and their eyes meet for a brief second. He stares at the struggling German just long enough to see the suffering in his eyes.

Gatenby leaps up from the saddle feeling as if he is screaming inside, and stamps down on the pedals as hard as he can. He turns and looks over his shoulder and stares for a moment into the eyes of his rival. Then he faces forward and his eyes close, and he begins to feel his chest starting to explode, and the muscles of his legs burn. Through his ear piece he can hear his boss telling him 'Two metres, five, ten, you've got him – he's dying, you've killed him – go, go'

Almost as one, everyone in the Cafe des Arcades and, a thousand miles away, in the Coach and Horses, stand up and start shouting...

Back on the mountain again and Gatenby takes a look over his shoulder – no rider in sight, just a screaming, baying crowd of spectators, and then a motorbike. *Where is he?* He looks ahead again and tries to block out the pain, counting every stroke – *one two, one two, one two.* He vaguely sees a figure running alongside his right shoulder and suddenly recognises English being shouted in his ear, 'Go on son, go on, you've got him, just keep going...' Then it's gone and the sound of the crowd melts back into one. Ahead the road is narrowed by the funnel of spectators, and he can feel them pouring water over his head and sometimes he bounces off them as they lean into the road and scream and shout. He longs for each and every hairpin so he can get a few seconds respite from the brutal incline. Each time he turns he has to stand on the pedals again to regain his momentum. Finally he looks to his left and sees his rival struggling up the crowded road below – the gap is growing. Can he allow himself to think he's done it? *'Must keep going, mustn't ease up, need to drink, need to breathe...'*

David Duffield is screaming and shouting *'Surely now Sean this is it, he's going to take the stage, he's going to take yellow and I think he's going to take the tour! This is fantastic, I don't know what to say, I've got a lump in my throat, in all my years in the sport I have never seen anything like this...'*

'I think you're right David, if he wins today there's nothing Ulrich can do to get this back, there are no more mountain stages and no time trial, so its all down to today'.

The tension rises in the cafe, in the pub in England, and in the mind of Gatenby as he struggles towards the summit. Hairpin ten, then eventually hairpin nine, *'surely now it's done'.* Hairpin eight – *'surely that should be seven?'* When he looks over the side of the road, he can see Ulrich, struggling, two or three bends below, his pink jersey blown open by the wind and his head bobbing from side to side.

He really has beaten him, he must keep going, keep stamping as hard as he can, keep breathing, keep feeling the burning, aching agony of every stroke of the pedals. Bend five, the village, bend four, three, two, the view of the mountainside briefly opens up ahead of him, past the chalets, into the shade of the hotels, downhill now. Breathe. Breathe. Breathe. Look up, enjoy the moment, fasten jersey (don't forget the sponsors), sit up, arms aloft, the finish line, the crowd, falling, breathing, the arms of the helper, the end.

Long into the night, there is celebrating in Cafe des Arcades and in the Coach and Horses, and time after time, the revellers have to explain to curious onlookers what all the fuss is about, as they order another drink and toast 'our boy', the hero of the hour, the man who tomorrow will be pulling on a yellow jersey and setting off towards Paris, towards a great victory, towards his own moment in history...

And as Gatenby begins to drift off to sleep, he opens his eyes one last time to savour the moment, and realises that he was struggling over the top of Norwood Edge, North Yorkshire (with its single hairpin half way up), and tries to imagine what it would really be like to have lived that moment as a younger man, to have beaten Ulrich, and to have fallen asleep that night wearing a Yellow Jersey, looking forward to a life in the fast lane, BBC sports personality of the year, and a slot on a chat show where he'll have to explain, not for the first time, why cyclists shave their legs.

And so it is that every boy who has ever kicked a football about in the park has dreamed that he is really at the world cup final, smashing home the winning goal into the top corner of a bulging net. And every child who has ever driven his parents mad belting a tennis ball against the wall of their house, likes to think he is scoring match-point at Wimbledon. But *they* can't do that. Because *they* can't just throw their kit in a bag and turn up at Wembley or the All England club and have a play about, in place of their heroes. Cycling is different. Cyclists *can* go and ride the exact same roads, and follow exactly in the wheel tracks of their heroes, and suffer every metre of tarmac under the same scorching sun. Then they can all go home, watch the real thing on television, and say, 'I've done that'.

My first memories of wanting to 'do that' go back to the mid-nineteen seventies when cycling was a minority sport in the UK, which seems hard to believe considering the recent boost in its popularity. The only time it was ever on television was on ITV, on 'World of Sport'. The tour de France would make a brief appearance on a feature called 'Sports Special One', which was a ten minute slot dedicated to minority sports. It came on after the wrestling – sporting giants like Giant Haystacks and Big Daddy battling it out in front of a crowd of screaming grannies who would do their best to belt the fighters with handbags and umbrellas as they lay pinned to the canvas of the ring.

During the Tour, mum and dad would sometimes let me carry my lunch through to the lounge and eat it on my lap whilst I watched the race. I remember the commentators talking about the 'first major climb of the day' – a phrase that stuck in my mind throughout the afternoon as I rode around the estate where we lived, riding up hills while rocking from side to side just like the pros did on the television. Of course, to find proper 'major climbs' my friends and I had to venture a bit further than the leafy lanes of suburbia, and slowly our range extended out into the Yorkshire Dales. The ultimate trip came when as a twelve year old me and my pal David Burnett spent three days youth hostelling. It rained solidly and we phoned home every night, but I loved it. We certainly found some 'major climbs', but walked up every single one of them pushing our bikes.

Then, as now, cycling was just as commercialised as any other sport and riders would be covered in sponsor's logos. Not wanting to be left out, I cut down a pair of jeans to the same length as a pair of cycling shorts, and scrawled 'Puch' along the bottom (because I had a Puch Pathfinder bike) – just like the pros, and then chose my most cycling-top-like t-shirt to wear. The fact that it said 'Berkley' on the front and not 'Molteni' like the one

Eddy Merckx wore didn't bother me one bit. I was going to be like those pros eventually, so may as well start now. I'm not the first wannabe to do this – when the legendary British rider Tommy Simpson was still a junior racer he got some shirts made up for him and his mates with 'Scala' written on them to make himself look more continental. There is a long culture of this sort of thing in British Cycling – a desire to bring ourselves closer to the heroes in Europe. There are many clubs who don't call themselves anything as mundane as 'York Cycling Club', opting instead for the much more exotic sounding 'Velo Club York'. British bike builders often give their bikes Italian sounding names. Ellis Briggs, the long established bike business hand build 'Favori' frames, even though they're based in Shipley, an old textile town in West Yorkshire.

As I got a bit older I began to understand that ink covered shorts and a cheap t-shirt didn't turn you into the next sporting superstar. Like all heroes, I began my long journey to the top by saving my pocket money for a new bike. I can't really remember running many errands, and can't claim to have suffered down a coal mine in order to scrape together the cash, but I did have a piece of A4 paper on which I had drawn a kind of thermometer that showed how much money I had saved. We moved house to a village in East Yorkshire and I set up a round selling kindling door to door. It was the perfect operation – I didn't do much of the hard work and creamed off most of the profits. It really relied on the fact that my Grandad would come and stay with us for the weekend, and to fill his time he would sit in our garage chopping off-cuts of roof joists into kindling that I would deliver. I needed a bike more than ever because I had started cycling to school, a journey of about three miles each way, so my little three speed 'racer' wasn't really up to the job. Eventually the day arrived when my dad came home with a ten speed Carlton in the back of his car. It had cost seventy-nine pounds. My future was assured – I was on my way and I had the gear to match.

The next stage of my journey was the day when I first met Dicco on the stairs at school. He stopped me to say that I'd probably get the pump stolen off my bike if I left it in the bike sheds. I don't know why we were all so worried about getting the pumps stolen off our bikes. I never knew of it happening to anyone, and no one seemed to be going around trading in cheap pumps to replace the stolen ones. From that moment on Dicco and I became friends. He was just like me in the fact that he too believed he was destined to reach the giddy heights of elite professional cycling, so we had a lot in common. We were two souls misunderstood by everyone around us. Everyone, that is, apart from Mr. Curtis, our careers teacher, who managed to keep a straight face when we put 'professional cyclist' in the 'What would you like to do when you leave school?' bit of the form he gave us one day. When it came to choosing our 'O' levels we made sure we took French – you needed to speak French if, like us, you were going to live in France and be a pro-cyclist.

We also had a PE teacher who actually let us leave school during PE lessons to go cycling. Mr. DeVries only asked for a letter from our parents. My dad pointed out that because I was so poor at any other sport it would only be a waste of everyone's time to make me attempt to kick a ball straight or do a decent job of bowling at cricket. I still can't play ball sports, and remember the humiliation of being picked last for every game of football that I have ever taken part in. This even happened a couple of years ago when I started going for a kick about with a few of the regulars from a pub in a village up the road from where I live. As the teams were picked, I would watch as everyone was picked before me, and I would humbly take my place in line with whichever team captain had the misfortune to realise I was the only person left. And this at the standard of football played by a bunch of wheezing overweight drinkers. So, with permission gained from our parents, Dicco and I would get let out of school during the afternoons. This would have been a golden opportunity for a good bit of skiving, but that was an opportunity we never took – we were too obsessed with riding our bikes. We would regularly endure the taunts of our school mates as we put on our cycling kit and they all got ready to go and spend their time on the patch of mud that passed as the school football pitch.

Over our teenage years, Dicco and I planned our route to the very top. Back then there were no scientific training methods so we just rode our bikes for as long and as far as we could. For hours on end we rode the windswept roads around East Yorkshire, dreaming of great victories to come. Every road was, in our minds, a replica of some part of Europe. Arras Hill, between Market Weighton and Beverley, was our own Mont Ventoux, and any potholed road was the 'Hell of the North' in deference to the early season races we knew we were destined to ride in Belgium. And as we rode to meet the Hull Thursday Road Club for their regular Sunday run, we knew that the trees that shaded our backs weren't on the main road towards the North Bar in Beverley, but were lining the Champs Elysees, and we knew in our heart of hearts that we were about to take Britain's first ever win in the Tour de France.

We would spend hours reading cycling magazines, dreaming of owning ever more exotic machinery, and make a nuisance of ourselves by hanging around in Cliff Pratt's bike shop in Hull. We wanted our bikes to be just like the ones the pros rode, and would cut and file and strip them down to make them at least look the part. The day Dicco got his first new bike, a Carlton Cyclone, it was fitted with what the catalogue described as 'racing mudguards'. These tiny little strips of aluminium didn't guard the rider from any mud, and certainly didn't help you go any faster. Naturally, the first thing Dicco did was to remove them and throw them away. When his mum saw how he had already defiled his lovely new bike, she was so mad with him that she wouldn't let him go out. In another attempt to make my bike more professional looking, I decided to respray it, and managed to cover everything in my dad's garage (including his motorbike) in a dusting of red spray paint. Naturally he was a bit angry, and despite my denials of any knowledge of how any of this had happened, and despite the newly acquired red colour on my mum's hair-dryer (I was in a rush to get the paint dry), I am still reminded of this incident regularly, even though it was over thirty years ago.

Eventually Dicco and I did get decent bikes – both the same

'Carlton Professional' frames which we built up bit by bit, and tried to equip to look just like the ones ridden by two local professionals called Sid Barras and Keith Lambert.

We raced all over the place and had careers only memorable by the lack of the professional contract that we craved. (Although it should be said that a few years later, Dicco did start to do quite well in some local races, but still failed to get himself spotted by any talent scouts from Europe. He still races today, and has a few wins to his credit). We spent all our money on trying to find ways to go faster. Dicco once bought some silk racing tyres, then the first time he used them, he got a puncture on the way to the start line at a race on the old Dam Busters base in Lincolnshire, so he hacked them to bits with a pair of scissors in anger.

Despite strenuous denials to our schoolmates and parents, we took to shaving our legs, probably even before we'd started to shave our chins. We were always in search of those few precious seconds that we thought stood between us and glory, we occasionally (very occasionally) would try to eat like an athlete – forfeiting chips, and trying to eat as many carbohydrates as we could, even though we didn't actually know what a carbohydrate was (and not realising that chips are, in fact, a form of carbohydrate). Still, we'd read somewhere that it was what the professionals did, so we did it too. We'd have exactly the same attitude to bits of equipment, always poring over magazines to see what latest bit of kit the pros were using. As one of the older, slightly cynical men who worked in Cliff Pratt's bike shop once said 'you lot would tow bloody chrome wheelbarrows behind your bikes if you saw some pillock doing it on the tour'.

Cycling clothing was going through a big change at this time as well. This was about the time that Lycra was invented. Up until then cycling jerseys were made of silk, and the shorts were usually made of a wool mix with a chamois leather insert to protect your nether region from saddle sores. Obviously this made them quite high maintenance – every time you washed your shorts you were supposed to rub lanolin into the chamois leather. We didn't have any lanolin so I used to pinch my dad's E45 cream, which he used against eczema on his hands. The other problem with old fashioned shorts was their ability to absorb vast amounts of water, which not only made you about a stone heavier every time it rained, but also meant that every time you stood up in the saddle, if your shorts were wet they would fall down around your knees. The only solution to this was to wear braces under your jersey, which presented yet more opportunity for ridicule from those unfamiliar with the needs of an aspiring professional cyclist. These days we are blessed with modern fabrics that can be easily washed and cared for; lanolin and braces are consigned to the pages of history.

At this point I might be expected to reach the part in the story where my dreams of a career as a top level athlete are shattered by injury. Just as I was about to pick up the pen to sign the contract that would see me heading off to Europe to race, win, and cover myself in glory, some mishap ends it all for me. On that final training run a wet patch of road saw me sliding on my back into a ditch, twisting a joint in the wrong direction and then not recovering enough to realise my full potential. Then I had to go back to school, do some work, and then get a 'proper' job. The rest of my life would be full of bitter resentment that I never saw the results of all my efforts, and I could only jealously sit watching cycling's occasional appearances on the television wondering what might have been.

It wasn't actually like that. My pal Paul Bennett got an electric guitar and rock and roll started to look like more fun than cycling, so I had a typical teenage change of direction, and didn't ride a bike for over twenty years.

The other consequence of my change of heart from cycling to electric guitar was that I gradually lost touch with Dicco. Our family moved away again, and I would only occasionally see him in a pub, and say a quick 'hello'.

Stage 2
A Big Idea

On November 20th, 1902 a journalist called Geo Lefevre met his editor, Henri Desgrange, at the Cafe de Madrid in Paris, to talk about an idea he had for a great bike race – a true 'Tour of France' that would be a great test of endurance for anyone who took part. Desgrange was looking for a way to boost circulation of his newspaper 'L'Auto', and Lefevre seemed to have hit on just the sort of idea he was looking for. They can hardly have known that by the time they had finished their lunch, they would have come up with an idea for a race that would grow to become the biggest annual sporting event in the world. The following January they announced their idea to the press, and in July of that year, the riders were ready to take the start.

If you ask most people to name as many bike races as they can, they'll probably have to stop after naming one – the very one created by Lefevre and Desgrange in November 1902 - The Tour de France. Almost everyone has heard of it and has a vague idea of what it is. Ask them to name anyone who has won it and they will probably mention Lance Armstrong, Bradley Wiggins and Chris Froome. If they are in their forties or a bit older, they may have heard of a Belgian called Eddy Merckx. Although a lot of people will only have heard of him because he went on to have his name painted on the type of 'racer' that most children rode to school, usually having taken off the drop handlebars and replacing them with wide cow-horn style ones to make the bike look more like a motorbike (a playing card in the spokes of the rear wheel to make a noise was another popular addition).

Much has changed since the first Tour de France (or 'the Tour' as anyone who considers themselves to know anything about it will call it), but one relic still visible from that era today is that if you look closely at the leader's Yellow Jersey (more of that later), you will see the initials 'HD' embroidered on it – this is in reference to Henry Desgrange, who has taken the credit for the idea since his meeting with Lefevre in the Cafe de Madrid. The races that Dicco and I used to drool over bare little resemblance to the original, but the basic concept is the same – a race through France, covering huge distances, with one eventual winner. Desgrange actually said that in the ideal Tour, there wouldn't just be one eventual winner, but just one eventual *finisher*.

The first race started on the Route de Corbeil, Paris on July 1st. For the first stage (there were six in all), the riders had to ride from Paris to Lyon. If you look on a modern map you can see that it is a long way from Paris to Lyon – even by the most direct motorway. I have driven that stretch of road, and even in a modern air conditioned car it's a serious journey, usually involving a couple a decent breaks, and possibly even a quick nap. For the first stage of the first Tour riders had to cover a whopping 467km or 290 miles, about the distance from London to Newcastle, on rough roads, on a primitive bike heavy enough to break a bone should you be unlucky enough to drop it on your foot. And just to really make it hard it had to be done without any form of outside assistance, unlike the fleet of mechanics and back up vehicles available to today's riders if they need any help with a mechanical breakdown, or just somewhere to put a discarded jersey.

This 'no outside assistance' rule probably had its most famous application in 1913. Frenchman Eugene Christophe was descending the Col de Tourmalet when his front forks snapped. This can only have resulted in the sort of crash that would, in modern times, go on to feature in the sort of 'When sports go bad' type of montage that is the staple diet of many cable television networks. Undeterred, Christophe dusted himself down and carried his bike to the village of St. Marie de Campan and knocked on the door of the local blacksmith. He then used the forge to repair his bike before rejoining the race. Unfortunately, he allowed the blacksmith's apprentice to work the bellows for him, thus incurring the wrath of the judges, who, in a classic piece of 'jobs worth' thinking, decided that this constituted 'outside assistance', and penalised him by adding ten minutes to his time for the day, even though he had lost four hours already as a result of his crash.

There are no such legendary incidents recorded from the first tour, which after arriving in Lyon at the end of the first stage (taking the fastest rider twenty-seven hours and forty-seven minutes), eventually finished back in Paris. There were no mountains in those days (well, not on the route of the Tour anyway), but the challenge was still huge and only twenty-one of the sixty starters got to the finish. A little short of the attrition that Henri Desgrange saw as the ideal, but a very high drop out rate nevertheless.

Eventual winner of that very first tour, Maurice Garin, came back to defend his title the following year, but somewhat spoiled his entry into cycling's hall of fame by making use of the French railway system to make sure he got back to Paris before anyone else. His disqualification was probably a much fairer interpretation of the 'no outside assistance' rule than when it was applied to the unfortunate Eugene Christophe.

In 1905, the tour continued to develop its reputation for controversy (which has continued until the present day), when Louis Trousselier decided he'd have a go at victory. The fact that he was supposed to be in the army at the time didn't dent his ambition. He simply went AWOL for the duration of the race. His superiors decided to let him off from any punishment because he won, probably realising that it would have made them look bad to punish a soldier who had just become a national hero. Trousselier went out for a bit of a celebration with his prize money, and lost the lot in a gambling den. One of the ways he concocted to get some of his hard earned money back was the 'dinner sprint'. This simple idea involved Trousselier and a bunch of his cycling friends arriving at a restaurant and ordering the finest food and wine. The owners were no doubt quite pleased to have such a famous and heroic customer, and obliged him and his party with the best they had to offer. When it came to the bill, the group would argue about who's turn it was to pay, and when the owners intervened, they would then decide that the only honourable thing to do was to settle the dispute like gentlemen and have a race – once around the block, and last one back would pay up. The owner would act as starter to ensure fair play and wave them off. That was of course, the last anyone would see of Trousselier and his friends.

One of the most iconic symbols of the Tour is the yellow jersey, or 'malliot jaune'. This is awarded to the overall leader each day, based on the cumulative time taken to cover each stage, added together to give an overall time for the distance covered so far. There is some debate as to when the jersey first appeared. It seems hard to believe that all the historians of cycling can't agree on such an important date, almost as if no one can quite remember when the FA cup final was first played. The Belgian multiple tour winner Philippe Thys said that he could remember being asked to wear a yellow jersey to mark him out as the leader in 1913, and as no one else has any memory or record of anything different, this date will probably become the accepted version of reality. It is generally accepted though, that it is yellow to match the colour of the paper that the sporting daily L'Auto was printed on. Any rider who has ever spent a day wearing the yellow jersey will be forever defined by that achievement, always being known as 'former yellow jersey holder...'. You can buy replicas in cycling shops the world over these days, but although there always seem to be plenty for sale, I don't ever remember seeing anyone wearing one. Personally, I wouldn't have the gall to ride around pretending to be the leader of the Tour de France, and get the feeling that anyone who does wear a yellow jersey is asking for ridicule at the very least, and to be ridden into the ground by all and sundry in any case. It's a bit like walking around school with a 'Kick me' sign stuck to your back.

This was one of the reasons that riders were originally not very happy with the idea. When Desgrange asked the leaders to wear the yellow jersey in order to make them stand out from the other riders, this high visibility was the very reason that the riders didn't want to wear it. They felt that other riders would find it too easy to keep an eye on their every move. Ironically, the first wearer (if he is to be believed), Philippe Thys, was persuaded to bow to Desgrange's request by his manager for this exact reason – the jersey would stand out and give better publicity to his sponsors. This reluctance on the part of the riders of Thys's day is a stark contrast to the present era. Many riders will not only wear the jersey itself, but will supplement it with matching shorts, gloves and helmet, and even in some cases, a specially painted bike to complete the ensemble. The disgraced seven times Tour 'winner' Lance Armstrong has been said to book himself into hotels under the name 'Jonathan Mellow'. (Think about it - Jonathan Mellow = Johnny Mellow = Mellow Johnny, which sounds a bit like 'Malliot Jaune', which is French for Yellow Jersey). He now owns a bike shop in his home town of Austin, Texas called 'Mellow Johnny's bike shop'.

Despite the status that earning the right to wear the jersey carries, there have been a couple of occasions when riders have refused the honour. In 1971 Eddy Merckx was so much the favourite to win the tour that fans were not expecting the usual suspense and excitement that the race normally provided. Merckx was utterly dominant at the time – he was a man with an insatiable appetite for winning, who saw no reason to do anything less than crush his opponents. His hold over the sport was so complete that all the other riders made unofficial alliances in the race and worked together to try to beat him. By the time the race reached the Alpine resort of Orcieres-Merlette, Merckx was eight minutes forty-two seconds behind the leader, the brilliant Spanish climber, Luis Ocana. Across Provence, heading for the Pyrenees, Merckx and his team set a brutal pace and gained time on Ocana. Once in the Pyrenees, as the riders climbed the Col de Mente, the weather took a turn for the worse and conditions on the roads became treacherous. Descending the other side of the mountain, Merckx was in the lead with Ocana taking huge risks to keep up with him. Merckx lost control on a bend and Ocana, unable to avoid him, also fell. Merckx was first up, but as Ocana struggled to unclip himself from his bike, he was hit by Dutchman Joop Zootemelk, who had also lost control on the slippery road. Screaming in agony from displaced vertebra and massive internal bruising, Ocana had to be taken off the mountain by helicopter. Merckx was so shocked that he initially wanted to quit the race, but was persuaded to ride on after a late night talking-to from his manager and team mates. Once he had agreed to ride, he said that he would not wear a jersey that he had only won by default, and only began to wear the yellow jersey four days later after winning a stage from a group of riders who had broken away from everyone else.

Over thirty years later the Tour was going through another period in its long history when it was being dominated by one man. The reign of Lance Armstrong surpassed all who had gone before him; he had already won six tours, and was starting the 2005 event as firm favourite.

Armstrong was a popular global celebrity at the time, as yet to fall foul of his murky past. He was still seen as an inspiring cancer survivor, and was a constant target of the paparazzi because of his charity work and his relationship with rock singer Cheryl Crowe. He was aiming for his seventh successive win and had totally dominated the race for its last six editions. The first stage in 2005 was a nineteen kilometre time trial along the Atlantic coast from Fromentine to Noirmoutier-en-l'Ile. Time trials are known as the 'Race of Truth' because there is no room for tactics or the use of other riders to give shelter from the wind. The riders set off at one minute intervals, and as defending champion, Lance Armstrong was last man off, with his great rival, Jan Ullrich one minute ahead. Amazingly, Armstrong caught and passed Ullrich- meaning he had not only gained over a minute on his greatest rival, and the only man who he considered to be a threat, but he had dealt him what must have been a devastating psychological blow. It can only be imagined how Ullrich must have felt, he'd trained all year for this event and then on the very first day his greatest rival had crushed him in the most public of ways. It might not have helped him that the previous day he had smashed his head through the rear window of his team car when it had braked suddenly, whilst he was being paced on a high speed training ride. Despite this, Armstrong didn't win that day – that honour went to his fellow American David Zabriskie, a lesser known member of the CSC team.

Zabriskie held onto the yellow jersey for the next two stages, when the race arrived in Tours, ready for the team time trial to Blois. The team time trial is a rather bizarre interlude in the tour. This time, the teams set off as groups, riding as a unit to help one another keep up the highest speed possible. Riders take turns at the front – going absolutely flat out for a few seconds as they take their turn to break a path through the air for their team mates, before moving to one side and dropping to the back of the line to recover in time for their next turn as group leader. Viewed from above (as is often the case in the television coverage of the race), it looks like a well choreographed chain, rotating backwards, but moving forwards a tremendous speed. At it's best it's almost an art form.

On the day of the 2005 team time trial few people expected to see the Discovery team (led by Armstrong) get beaten, unless it was by CSC – the team containing yellow jersey wearer, Zabriskie. Although the yellow jersey was at stake, the rivalries between the two teams added another dimension to the day. Armstrong has always loved the team time trial and obviously wanted to win his final one, but CSC were viewed as a new powerhouse of the sport and didn't want to be seen as second best to the 'Disco boys', as Armstrong's team were called.

The two teams were the last two to start – Discovery ahead of CSC. Once the teams were on the road, the only way to tell who was winning was to look at the intermediate time checks along the course. Discovery was the fastest team throughout the early part of the course, but CSC was a team on a mission, and bettered even the formidable 'blue train' of the American team. As they neared the finish it began to look like Discovery was going to be beaten for the first time in years. CSC took the last bend into the President Wilson Avenue in Blois and accelerated towards the banner marking 'one kilometre to go'. As the line of riders shot forward, there was a sudden explosion of chaos in the middle of the line and unbelievably it was the yellow jersey that was sent sprawling. Zabriskie slid along the wet cobbles, tearing his clothing and stripping flesh from the left side of his body. His reign in the yellow jersey was over. He picked himself up and cycled in to the finish ninety seconds behind his team mates.

Lance Armstrong took over the yellow jersey that day, but the manager of the CSC team, Bjarne Riis was quoted as saying, 'The man in the Yellow Jersey is there because of luck'. Armstrong was furious, and on the morning of the next day he arrived at the start in his team kit, not the yellow jersey, as a gesture to salute the unfortunate Zabriskie. It may also have been a dig at Bjarne Riis, but whatever lay behind his actions, it was the same as Eddy Merckx had done all those years ago. Unlike Merckx however, the authorities stepped in, and Armstrong had to make a quick detour to dress as the organisers wanted him to, and as he rolled away from the start, he was in the *malliot jaune*.

Since the day that Lefevre and Desgrange finished their lengthy lunch and put the final touches to their idea for the Tour de France, it has grown into a huge annual spectacle, with a global following of millions. It has its own history, studded with characters and legends that only grow with time. It dominates France for three weeks every July. More than ten million people line the road sides to watch it, and it now comprises of a travelling entourage of over three thousand people as it winds it's way around France, creating new heroes and villains as it does so.

That myself and Dicco aren't amongst those heroes is something that I often think about, usually from the comfort of a sofa in front of the television. During those many hours I spent watching the race each year, I don't think those childhood dreams ever left me.

Stage 3
Coming Back From Nowhere

There are few more beautiful places than England in the spring, and even fewer, if any, that are nicer than Yorkshire in the spring.

This was the thought that crossed my mind as my family and I drove out of town to see our friend's new house in a village up in the Dales. As we turned off the main road, the lane swung to the left, and the whole of Nidderdale lay before us. It was a glorious patchwork of fields, dotted with houses and villages, framed by the moors and a clear blue sky. For some reason, I remembered how there would have been a time when I thought that this would be a perfect day for a bike ride. As ever, my wife was the first person to hear of this. She took it in the same spirit that she usually did when I shared another of my daydreams with her.

'It would be brilliant to ride a bike on this road', I said

'I don't know why you don't just get yourself a bike', she replied. I thought that she might just have a point.

There had been occasional times over the intervening twenty years since my last ride with Dicco that my love of cycling would begin to stir in me again. Sometimes I might walk past a bike shop and look inside and remember the times when Dicco and I would spend hours pestering the men who worked in Cliff Pratt's bike shop, asking to look at bits and pieces that we had no intention of buying, and showing off in front of the other (non 'proper' cyclist) customers, who were mostly parents who had come in to buy a shiny BMX bike for their eager children.

Other times I might watch the Tour de France on television,

offering my expert opinion to anyone who was unlucky enough to be in earshot, trying to explain the finer tactical points of what was going on. Despite this, I have little memory of top level cycling during those years, apart from the year Irishman Stephen Roche won the Tour, and my dad phoned me from France to tell me he had spent the evening with a friend of his from Dublin, called John Brown, and that they had drunk a whole bottle of Irish Whiskey, because John had taught maths to Stephen Roche when he was a young schoolboy.

I had even sold my beloved Carlton Professional – for £150 that I can't remember spending on anything in particular. The only remaining part of my life that ever suggested I had been a keen cyclist was the old club jersey which was kept in a suitcase at my parent's house. They eventually gave it back to me when they were having a clear out.

So, my life hadn't quite worked out as I had originally planned in my teens. Instead of finding myself in my mid-thirties, a retired pro-champion, married to a podium girl, doing the odd bit of television punditry and endorsing yet another line of bike frames and equipment, I was married to someone I'd met at work, gradually gaining a bit of weight, and occasionally thinking of telling my children of what might have been.

Maybe there always was an inkling of that old passion being re-awakened somewhere in the depths of my psyche. For years, the back of my wardrobe remained taken up with my old club jersey, folded and all but forgotten. Even so, little flashes of desire kept coming into my mind – I'd be driving along some bit of road somewhere and as my thoughts would begin to wander, I'd start to think about how nice it would be on a bike instead of being in a car. This only seemed to afflict me on the type of roads that make riding a bike such a pleasure- the traffic free, scenic, sun-drenched roads that climb over the moors around Yorkshire. I even started to look in bike shops again, although I very rarely ventured inside, in case someone got talking to me and I might have to face up to the fact that I'd lost interest in something that had once been so special, and that I was no longer 'a cyclist'.

There was, of course, a sense of inevitability to all this, and I'm sure I knew deep within myself that I would somehow, one day, start to ride a bike again. Ironically it was Dicco who finally laid to rest all the excuses I had been making to myself. He got back in touch with me through the internet, and we arranged to meet up again for the first time in over twenty years. He told me he was still cycling. We had met in a pub in Harrogate, and he was driving, so stuck to soft drinks. I was on foot, so a few rounds of drinks meant that I drank too much, and as the evening wore on, we began to reminisce about our old cycling days. He told me there was no excuse for me not cycling again. He even tried to sell me a bike, although thankfully I was still in control enough of my decision making processes not to buy it.

The next day I decided that there were to be no more excuses, no more procrastination, it was time to take the first steps to reignite my love of the bike. I reached into the back of my wardrobe, and took out my old Hull Thursday Road Club jersey. It even still fit me. That was it. I was going to start cycling again.

Firstly, of course, I needed a new bike. I was sure that I had some bits and pieces to go with that old club jersey, but no matter how much I routed around in the loft I couldn't find any of it so the shopping list of things needed to start my comeback was swelled by the need for gloves, shorts, a jersey (I wasn't actually going to wear my old one), and a helmet.

There was no debate about the need for a helmet, but in my previous cycling life no one ever wore one. Even when I raced time trials as a teenager there was no compulsion to take what is now considered as the most essential precaution. I find that quite hard to believe – the thought of someone organizing a race and then letting unsupervised teenagers hurtle around on public roads with no head protection. The people of todays legal profession would have been in seventh heaven at the limitless potential for lucrative cases. There would probably have been crowds of them at every difficult bend or potentially lethal road junction.

Part of the problem was that the helmets that were available were largely ineffective and referred to as 'hairnets'. They were constructed of padded straps of leather that looked like an up turned basket. The only time we were made to wear them (and consequently the only time we *did* wear them), was in circuit races. After one particularly painful, bike wrecking fall, Dicco's mum made him get one of the new hard shell helmets. These were made of fibreglass and supposedly gave much more protection, but were made even less popular than 'hairnets' by the fact that they generally became known as 'piss pots'. He was teased a lot about it and I don't really remember him wearing it much. But, back to the real job in hand, and looking for a new bike.

I was in a local branch of Halfords one day when my eyes settled on a bright yellow road bike. This might sound like some kind of fateful 'love at first sight' moment, but it was nothing of the sort. I was keen to buy a new bike and lacked the confidence to go into a bike shop and be the sort of ignorant customer I used to ridicule all those years ago in Cliff Pratt's outlet back in Hull. I was waiting to be seduced. It looked brilliant to me - oval frame tubes ('aerodynamic to cut through the air!') integrated levers ('work your brakes *and* your gears'), deep profile wheel rims ('aerodynamic again!') and an alloy frame ('amaze yourself with its light weight!'). I was very taken with it, and believed all the little bits of information on the card hanging from its handlebars. The truth was that it was simply twenty years more modern that the last bike I had ridden. It was a bit like comparing an original Mini to its modern equivalent. If my children get in a car that's more than ten years old, they are mystified by the window winders. When I was young it was only in luxury cars where you would find electric windows, air conditioning or even a basic radio. Now every car has them, and they are accepted as the norm - just like aerodynamic tubes, deep profile rims, integrated levers and lightweight alloy frames, but I didn't really consider this, because I had already been seduced by the modern look and bright yellow paint of a mid-range bike from Halfords.

What I should have done of course was carry out a bit of research and taken some advice. You're always told when you're looking for a car not to go and buy the first one you see, but that's more or less exactly what I did with my bike. My decision was slightly hurried by the fact that Halfords had a sale on and had knocked about seventy pounds off its price, and then made it even more tempting by the offer of fifty pounds worth of free gear if you spent over two hundred and fifty pounds. The reduced price of the bike was about two hundred and sixty pounds, so thanks to my Yorkshire 'don't spend money unless you have to' gene, it was simply too good to miss.

One return trip to Halfords later, I was set up – a new bike, a new jersey, a new helmet, and even a puncture repair kit. I paid my money and was told to come back later in the week to pick up the bike once it had been 'inspected'. The last time I had been excited like this was in the run up to Christmas as a child – probably whilst waiting for a new bike. Despite the fact that I sort of rushed into the purchase I was delighted, and apart from the other minor fact that it was a bit big for me, in the long run I got good service from that bike and it never let me down.

What I needed now was a route – somewhere to launch myself back into the world of cycling, but this time, without any dreams of sporting glory. There were no illusions – at nearly forty, I was about twenty years too old to do any more than try to get a bit fitter and slow down the ageing process. Even so, I didn't want to fall at the first hurdle so I did a bit of reconnaissance in the car. I took to taking slightly longer routes home and turning off the main roads to explore some of the country lanes that I normally paid no attention to as I went around on my day to day journeys for work. It's amazing how, when you make the effort, you can suddenly learn that the place you live is even nicer than you thought it was. I discovered seemingly endless pleasant winding side roads and picturesque little villages – all within few miles of where I live.

Apart from trying to find a reasonably flat route, the other problem was that there was now twenty years' worth of extra traffic on the roads. Gone were those empty rural roads of my youth, coupled with the fact that I now lived in a town, and not a village, so I had to consider the hazards of traffic and the ever worsening attitude of motorists to cyclists. Eventually I spotted a promising looking lay by on a country road just outside town, which would be ideal for setting off on my first ride, because it was on a road that could be part of a flattish circuit that was five point eight miles long (I had measured it in the car) – ideal for a first ride.

I can't pretend this was a glorious beginning. Five point eight miles is barely any distance at all, but the old mindset soon came back – an imaginary commentary running through my head, telling me that I was on the verge of yet another glorious mountain top victory somewhere in the Alps. In reality it was five, nearly six, almost entirely flat miles and I was suffering more than I can ever remember. I was quickly into my lowest gear and out of breath. There were one or two tiny undulations on the route and every one of them felt like a mountain. I just couldn't believe that twenty years of sloth had put me back so far. I couldn't believe that I was actually unfit. It was hard to imagine that those golden summers spent effortlessly pedalling for miles through the countryside were a reality and not just some kind of rose tinted memory.

I can remember the feeling of turning the pedals the first time I got back on that bike, on my very first ride. It was a pleasant enough sunny summer's evening, and I set off from that lay by just outside town. I flicked the pedal over and slid my foot into the toe clip (I was quite proud of the fact that I managed this simple task at the first attempt), and looked down at my feet turning the pedals. The years slipped away and I felt like I did all that time ago. It felt right. I had a genuine feeling of being in the place I was always meant to be. The traffic didn't really bother me and I was soon onto quieter roads. I remember rounding one corner and coming across a mobile fish and chip van. There I was, trying to undo years of laziness and I had temptation thrust in my face. Fortunately it was easy to resist the smell of frying chips, as I didn't have any money on me. I simply made bit of extra effort and glided past looking every inch the seasoned cyclist and tried my best not to look too self-righteous. Every little undulation on the ride was agony, but I was deliriously happy and I really didn't care.

So with my first excursion out the way, I knew I had to start pushing the boundaries and doing what we used to call 'getting the miles in'. I really took the phrase 'moderation in all things' as literally as possible, very gradually doing a bit more, even getting knocked off my bike by a careless teenager in a Fiat Uno, then eventually getting my mileage, and my average speed, up into double figures. Very quickly, I realised I was getting the old obsession back. Call it a truism, a cliché, or whatever you like, but it really was just like when you meet up with an old pal after twenty years and it feels like you only saw him last week. I became a cyclist once more. It filled my thoughts and became my dream, I wanted to ride more and go further and faster. I started to dream about a flashy new bike, and to wonder why I hadn't stuck at it all those years ago, and gone on to win the Tour de France.

A few weeks later I finally pedalled my way over that road with its stunning view over Nidderdale with the whole of the valley set out below me.

I had been planning to do my first 'long' ride for a while. This was an added aspect to my new hobby that I hadn't considered – I got the chance to spend hours poring over maps. Maps on the internet still weren't really available, and there was something satisfying about unfolding a paper map and spreading it out on the floor. I began to feel like I knew the whole of the area like the back of my hand, even though it was in a purely two dimensional way. Different roads and villages began to look tempting as places to ride through. I planned circuit after circuit, and was shocked to see how paltry the distances I had already covered looked. They barely took me from one fold of a map to another. This served as added incentive to make me do more miles.

After many hours of tracing and retracing routes on my map, I finally came up with a route for my first 'decent ride'. I'd leave home, cross over into Nidderdale and on into the Dales before blasting back down the valley and home again. This would surely leave me with a healthy glow, a feeling of self-righteous satisfaction, and the knowledge that I would have covered three or four folds of my map.

The day dawned perfectly – clear skies and not a breath of wind. I had a decent breakfast, but not the steak and pasta that my Tour de France heroes would have eaten all those years ago. I packed a couple of jam sandwiches into my pockets, filled up my one water bottle and set off. This really was ideal – the weather warm enough for me to only need short sleeves and no chance of rain.

I soon left the town behind and got onto quiet country lanes. The first few hills didn't feel too bad, I even managed to put on a decent turn of speed as traffic squeezed past me on some of the narrower roads. In my mind it wasn't hard to remember how all those years ago I would imagine that the cars and motorbikes going past were the TV and camera crews vying for position to film my great victory. In reality they were frustrated motorists being held up by a middle aged man doing his best to recapture his youth, much in the same way as the riders of high powered motorbikes that would blast past me every so often.

I felt like I was flying as I passed through village after village and then up the side of the very same reservoir that I had cycled passed as a twelve year old boy on my first youth hostelling trip. The hostel building was still there, but I noticed that it had changed into a holiday home. I reached the top of the reservoir and readied myself for that old commentator's cliché that I still remembered from the first time I watched the Tour de France on television, 'the first major climb of the day'.

I felt ready for it because I had fuelled myself with my two jam sandwiches. I wasn't even put off by the signs warning of a 'very steep ascent'. It didn't really occur to me that this was probably the first time I had seen a sign like this. I convinced myself that it really wouldn't be too bad. I clicked down into my lowest gear, made the right turn towards the hill and stamped on the pedals.

To say that I was unprepared for what followed would be an understatement similar to someone saying that 'Elvis could sing a bit'. The road reared up in front of me like a wall. It was so steep that the tarmac seemed as if it was only a few inches from my nose. When you climb a steep hill on a bike you very quickly go into 'oxygen deficit' and your breathing gets more and more difficult. Suddenly I was gasping for breath and felt like my eyes were going to pop out of my head. My legs felt like they were going to explode and I quickly realised that there was no way I was going to make it over the top. I just managed to unclip my feet from the pedals and avoid collapsing completely and looking stupid, managing instead to content myself with slumping over the handlebars and trying to breathe without being sick.

My eyes were streaming and I could barely see the odd car that chugged past up the hill. I knew I was going to have to face the ultimate indignity, and walk the rest of the way up. The problem was made worse by the fact that I had recently 'graduated' to using clip-less pedals. This meant that the slightly strange look that skin tight Lycra gives any middle aged man, even if he has started to feel a bit fitter, was made even more unusual by the fact I was trying to walk with cleats attached to the bottom of my shoes. Wearing cleats is fine whilst pedalling, but they make walking in cycling shoes very difficult. Especially up a twenty five per cent (one in four) hill like the one I was looking up now. I slipped and slithered my way to what I thought was the top of the hill before remounting and trying to ride on. I managed about thirty yards before I realised that just because the slope had eased, it hadn't eased enough for me to ride up it.

It took me about three attempts to finally get back on my bike and stay on it. The trouble was that there wasn't a huge sweeping descent to follow the climb, so my efforts had been a lot of pain for what felt alike absolutely no gain. Normally on television when one of my heroes like Eddy Merckx or Bernard Hinault got to the top of a mountain, they zipped up their jersey and set off down the other side, descending long sweeping roads for what seemed like ages, and a just reward for having fought their way up thousands of metres of Alpine pass. All that lay ahead for me that day was a bleak looking moorland with an undulating road running across it. It was even threatening to rain. Added to this was a stiff head wind which seemed to have sprung up since I left home, which meant I was really struggling. The road seemed to go on forever, and I kept stopping to look at the map to convince myself that I was going the right way. There was a bit of descent – the road dropped down by a reservoir, but the joy of this was soon taken away by yet another climb – but at least I managed to ride all the way up this time.

By the time I began to go back in the direction of home, with still about twenty miles or so to go, I was really in trouble. The two jam sandwiches I had 'fuelled up' with were long gone and I had to keep stopping at the side of the road to recover a bit before pressing on. Had I been called on for any kind of post ride analysis I'd have to admit that I hadn't eaten enough, and made the serious error of not bringing any money with me. I hadn't planned on stopping so had assumed I wouldn't need any. Every time I passed a shop I was tortured by the image of all the goodies I would have been able to go in and buy if only I had planned things better – a Mars bar and can of cola would have made all the difference to how I was feeling. Nowadays I eat a bowl of porridge and then some eggs on toast before I set out (because I read somewhere that that's what the pros do), but this was before I had read up on the idea of 'carbo-loading', and I had woefully underestimated the effects of my efforts. I also take some money, and even a credit card, just in case. When I eventually made it home, I was absolutely shattered, barely able to stand up, but the sense of achievement I felt was fantastic. I had finally done my first 'long one'.

After that my regular evening rides seemed easy. I had gained my own personal badge of honour in completing my 'long one', and felt like I could afford a few 'short ones' without compromising my ever increasing level of fitness. I was hardly a highly tuned athlete – but I noticed that the hills that used to leave me utterly breathless now just left me slightly out of breath.

As I walked back into our kitchen one day after one of my 'training' rides there was an unfamiliar lady sitting drinking tea with my wife. She was the mother of one of my son's friends from nursery. I was wearing my cycling kit, which, at my age, can best be described as unflattering, and was fairly well covered in grime.

I felt a need to explain my appearance to someone who wasn't familiar to what the best dressed cyclist wears in the early part of the twenty first century. 'I don't normally dress like this' I said. 'I've been cycling'.

Her name was Nicky and she told me that her husband was doing a charity bike ride later in the year, from Leeds to Scarborough. This was just the sort of thing I needed, so without thinking, I volunteered to join him. Nicky also said that her husband wasn't a cyclist. It struck me afterwards that she obviously thought I *was* cyclist – a 'proper' one who knew his stuff, and wore Lycra and could cover huge distances without breaking into a sweat.

Now I had another purpose to what I was doing. No longer was I just pedalling around aimlessly, dreaming of the days when Dicco and I used to pretend we were in the Tour de France. I was going to do a real bike ride – a whole hundred kilometres. (I had suddenly decided to think in metric because the distances always sounded further). I realised that I had better prove my worth as a proper cyclist by doing a decent job of it. I got in touch with a lady called Carol Robertson and offered to help plan the route. Nicky put me in touch with her husband Paul so I could offer my 'expert' advice to help him do the ride, because I was a 'real' cyclist and he hadn't ridden a bike since he was a boy. At last, it was all real again, I had convinced myself that I was a cyclist, and once I had met Nicky, I had convinced someone else that I was a cyclist too.

It felt as if the first part of the process I was going through was complete. I had finally overcome all the excuses and become a cyclist once more, giving myself some form of identity that went beyond everything else, and set me apart from other people. There are all sorts of things in life that combine to make you what you are, to give you a sense of purpose. Being a dad, being good to your loved ones, a good family man – they're all hugely important. But sometimes we all need to disappear into ourselves and do something that is entirely self-centred. In my case, I ride a bike, and once I set off, I'm in a world of my own. I ride a bike. That's what I like to do. I just wish it I could do it more often.

Stage 4
Dedication and Obsession

Now that I had become 'a cyclist' once more, and had a goal to aim for – albeit a modest 100km ride, I began to view my cycling a bit differently. This was probably something I should really have tried to have avoid – I hadn't intended on developing an obsession.

Most sports people share their lives with someone – wife, husband, whoever, and it varies as to how the other half of this relationship thinks of their loved one's pastime. Do they think 'he's very dedicated' or 'he's obsessed with that bloody bike'? We all admire the dedication of the successful elite athlete – but if we had to live with someone like that on a day to day basis would it drive a normal person to distraction? Tommy Simpson was one of Britain's greatest ever cyclists, but in his early life girls were put off because he only ever talked about cycling. Lance Armstrong describes in his auto biography how he would spend time weighing out every portion of his food – which amongst other carefully measured out substances, contributed to his achievements, but can hardly have added to the atmosphere of a family meal with his wife and children.

I was talking to an old friend of mine once who runs a pub football team. This is at the sort of level where a bunch of over-weight men turn up every Sunday to a wet field and play football without any chance of glory or recognition. One of the main qualifications to play at this level is to own a car - If you give a few team mates a lift, you get to choose what position you play. To most people this would sound like a completely unappealing way to spend a Sunday morning, but these people do it because they love it. They get immense pleasure from the game itself, nothing else. He described the dedication of his players not only by the fact they stuck at it and turned up to play every week, but by the fact that most Saturday nights they cut down on their drinking to minimise the effects of over indulgence the next day. In reality 'cut down on their drinking' meant they had seven pints instead of eight, but nevertheless, they were making a small sacrifice for the sake of their sport.

At the other end of the scale I once read an article by a retiring professional cyclist. He described how soon after he retired, he realised that he could now enjoy his food without feeling guilty. He said that in the whole of his *ten year* professional career there had only been *two or three days* when he hadn't thought about every single thing he ate or drank and how it might affect his cycling. I think I've done well if I manage to restrict my alcohol intake to weekends only, and think I've done even better if I keep the beers to a minimum the night before I'm planning a ride. So, the difference in dedication between me and a top professional is that I can manage five nights off the beer, and this chap managed ten years of self-discipline. I sometimes wonder just how fit I could really get if I showed the same level of application, then realise that all the abstinence, training and careful weighing of food portions would only make me so unhappy that I would be too miserable to want to ride my bike.

In my case I tried not to become too obsessed – I was only starting to go out on my bike a couple of evenings each week, but I noticed that I didn't view this any longer as 'going for a ride'. I started to think of it as 'training'. I had reached the top of that slippery slope that is the beginning of an obsession. Even so, my level of dedication wasn't having much of an effect on my life.

To try and make sure I was doing things right I started to read up on training methods and advice. There is a wealth of information available nowadays, all of which seemed mainly to serve as a means of providing me with something else to prove how inadequate I was. It was a stark contrast to the advice that had been available to me and Dicco in our early days, which could be summed up in the phrase 'Just ride your bloody bike '.

I discovered that my body fat was 18%, I weighed about 72kg, my resting heart rate was about sixty, and my body mass index was 23. I really had no idea of the relevance of these numbers, but thought I would try to put them into context by comparing them to people I saw regularly in cycling magazines that I was now reading. I found out that the Italian rider Paulo Bettini, at the time he was both World and Olympic champion, was considered to have quite a high body fat percentage at eight per cent, and Lance Armstrong (body fat 'between three and four per cent') had a resting heart rate often quoted to be around 32. Still, on the bright side, a good few pro-riders are heavier than me and I had a similar body mass index to Eddy Merckx, so at least I wasn't completely unfit for the task ahead. In the same way that beauty and lifestyle magazines seem to do nothing more for their readers than convince them that are ugly and leading rubbish lives, fitness magazines just showed me how unfit I really was.

Up until this point in my life I had a pathological loathing of gyms and 'fitness centres'. I can remember taking one of my children to a birthday party in a big rented room at one of these places near home. This just further reinforced my attitude. I hated the distant smell of physical exertion and the people strutting around in skin tight t-shirts that looked like they had been sprayed on. I hated the adverts for sessions on self-improvement and for various 'cleansing' processes that were intended to undo all the excesses for modern life. I thought I didn't need them – after all I thought I was neither unfit nor over weight. Well, not very unfit, I would only get a bit out of breath if I had to run anywhere. All this started to change the day I went from 'riding my bike' to 'going out training'.

With winter approaching I decided I didn't want to lose any of my fitness in the 'off season' so I went to a gym and tentatively enquired about membership. A young man showed me around whilst trying to convince me that spending the sort of money I usually save up for a family holiday was 'good value'. He told me that I only had to go 'three or four times a week' and my membership would pay for itself. That didn't sound like much – 'three or four times a week' but once I realised that this would mean only staying in for one evening during the week, or giving up a chunk of my weekend, which is a bit difficult when you have a family, then the unreality of it started to sink in. Then when I thought about going three or four times a week *every week* for fifty two weeks a year the reality started to dawn on me. I travel a bit on business, there's family stuff to get in the way, and we go on holiday sometimes. The cost suddenly started to look very expensive.

So instead I went to our local leisure centre to find out about 'spinning'. Being born and bred in Yorkshire, it was second nature for me to work out that paying per lesson was going to be much cheaper, especially as I was, in reality, unlikely to go two or three times a week for fifty two weeks a year.

There were a few of these spinning sessions a week at the leisure centre so I could go more or less when I wanted. 'Spinning' is part of the modern day phenomenon of fitness – where you go to a place, to pay good money to have someone inflict pain on you and yell at you at the same time. What really happens is that you sit on a stationary bike in a steamy hot room, in the dark, to the sound of loud music and surrounded by people in various states of fitness. Some of these people are in such states of physical perfection that they add to the pain by making you feel inadequate. Others look like they're about to breathe their last breath and make you try to remember your first aid training, just in case they keel over half way through. I had been told by the nice lady on reception that all I needed to take was a drink and a towel. I turned up ready for my first session. As we filed in I became conscious that I was the only man. This left me with a bit of a quandary. I didn't want to sit near the front and raise expectations that I was going to try to out-perform everyone, so I had made my way to the bike at the very back of the class. Then I realized that this might just have made me look like I wanted to stare at a load of lady's back sides. But it was too late to move, and it hadn't been easy to set the bike up to fit me, so I stayed put.

Once the class got underway I had yet another lesson in learning about suffering. I tried to keep up with the instructor, wipe away the sweat, not look at ladies bums, adjust the bike, but still the pain just got worse and worse. By half way through I felt just as bad as I ever had on any bike ride. This was serious agony. I kept looking at the clock, willing it on to the end of the forty minute session, but no matter how many times I looked, time just seemed to pass more and more slowly.

By the time the end finally came there must have been about three pints of sweat on the floor and splattered all over the bike. The instructor gave us a collective pat on the back and made us give ourselves a round of applause. I hurriedly put my tracksuit back on to cover the huge sweat patches that were all over me. We were all given a spray and huge piece of tissue paper to wipe our bikes (and in my case the surrounding ten square feet of floor), and departed with a promise of an even harder session next time. I wasn't sure what to think. Working on the basis of 'No pain, no gain' then the session had obviously done me a load of good, but I still felt that I didn't really fit in to the gym scene. After all, I was a spindly legged almost forty year old trying to get fit for a bike ride. Proper gym users wear tight t-shirts and like nothing better than to tell you about how much iron they can bench press and how many push-ups they can do in half an hour.

My reticence had been increased even further the first time I saw the instructor. She was one of the fittest looking people I had ever seen - she didn't appear to have an inch of fat anywhere on her, and never seemed to break into a sweat. After I limped out from my first spinning session I was shocked to see her happily welcoming another group of people straight after us, and realised that she was about to do the whole thing again. She probably didn't break into a sweat then either. But, she had an ability to cajole the group into pushing themselves that extra mile (or inch in my case), and I became a regular at her sessions. There's always a sound track to a spin session – usually some bass heavy dance music of the sort you usually hear coming from a Vauxhall Astra with blacked out windows, but Claire seemed about the same age as me so we were occasionally treated to The Clash or something similar which was a big help to me in overcoming my physical inability to keep up with the pace of the session. So, after a few nervous and exhausting attempts, spinning became a part of what I had started to call my 'regime'.

My twice weekly spinning sessions began to fit quite nicely into my routine and I started to feel the benefit pretty quickly. Then came a dawning realisation that there had been yet another fundamental change in my outlook – I had become a regular user of the gym. I tried to hold onto the belief that I wasn't like all the other body building gym users who bore their friends rigid by talking about 'pectoral development', but I did find myself telling people how good spinning was. This was beginning to get serious.

One problem with a solo approach to training is that you don't have any one to gauge yourself against. I had the feeling I was getting fitter and began to notice that my rides were getting a bit easier, but that didn't really tell me anything. Unfortunately most of the other cyclists I saw on the road either flew past me from behind, or came the other way cruising along effortlessly. At least I had got to the point where I could give the impression to people coming the other way that I was also cruising along with hardly any effort. My ambition of spotting another cyclist up ahead, then catching and passing them was still unfulfilled at this point.

Dicco and I were in sporadic contact by now and we arranged to go for a ride. This would be the first time in over twenty years that we had ridden together. The last time we went out we were still dreaming of our future in the world of professional cycling, we were young, fit, and could blast along at about the same speed. In fact, I was probably a bit quicker than he was. I had been back on the bike for only a couple of months and the paltry mileage I had notched up in that time was all I had done in twenty years, and I was riding a mid-range bike from Halfords. Dicco had had a lay off but had already been back to race fitness for quite some time. He had even passed the age old benchmark of getting under the hour for a twenty five mile time trial. This achievement has long been the aim of many British club cyclists, and I never even attempted it, never mind got close to it. It is actually a pretty serious thing to do – to average over twenty five miles per hour for a whole hour. I have often wound myself up to that speed when I've been out on my own. It's not that difficult to get up to twenty five miles an hour, but it is very hard to keep going at that speed for any length of time, and even harder if you're on your own. The twenty five mile time trial is a peculiarly British event. Riders race over a meticulously measured course, usually around dawn, and must ride the whole thing without sheltering behind one and other. It's a very pure test of speed and stamina.

The ride I had planned for Dicco and I was nowhere near that distance. I had decided on a little circuit that I had done myself a few times which took in a couple of scenic villages. We drove out, parked in a hotel car park and got ready to set off. I helped him get his bike of out his car. I couldn't believe how light it was.

'That's my Pinarello Prince', he said. I think he was quite proud, but at the time the name didn't mean anything to me. Since then I've come to learn what he meant and why he was so proud of it. It was the cycling equivalent of a Maserati, and when I looked at it I realised it was stunningly beautiful, perfectly proportioned and felt to be about half the weight of my bike. I like to think that my total lack of fitness had nothing to do with the fact that Dicco left me trailing within the first mile, and that it was my heavy bike that meant he could disappear into the distance every time the road went vaguely up hill. The extra weight theory was disproved when he gained even more ground when we went downhill.

The truth was that it was yet another rude awakening about how unfit I was. It was great to ride with Dicco again and the years slipped away, just like Dicco did – into the distance. I tried my hardest to stay close to his back wheel – just like a struggling pro would do, to take advantage of the slip steam of a rider in front of him, but I couldn't even do that. I wasn't disheartened, it had been brilliant to ride with someone else and I just felt even more like riding my bike. I even had a new target – trying to keep up with Dicco. Or at least being overtaken less often when I was out on my own.

As the evenings got lighter, I began to take advantage by going out for an hour or so after work. I was still in the habit of loading the bike into the car and trying to find a scenic bit of road to ride along because I still wasn't keen on riding in heavy traffic. This was a result of a disagreement a Fiat Uno. I had been happily riding out of town when I saw it come out of a junction to my right, heading straight across in front of me, trying to get into a side road on my left. I knew straight away that the driver hadn't seen me. I also knew I was about to get knocked off my bike for the first time ever. As is often described in these situations, time seemed to slow down and I had time the think to myself, 'I spent years cycling as a kid and this never happened'. I had time to raise my hands in front of my face to preserve my looks before the car smacked into me, sending me sprawling into the road.

Because it was a low speed impact, I was shaken more than hurt. I jumped up, grabbed my bike and got myself out of the way of the oncoming traffic. I was furious and was readying myself for a confrontation with the driver. After all it was a result of total carelessness (as is usually the case in these situations), so I had a right to be angry. The door of the car opened and a teenage girl appeared who was already almost in tears. I couldn't possibly be angry with her, so, as calmly as I could, I told her she should be more careful. She was obviously scared stiff about what had happened. She didn't even know that we were supposed to swap insurance details, so I asked her for her name and address which she wrote out for me and I gave her my number as well. She seemed almost as bothered about what her dad was going to say as anything else. Luckily I wasn't hurt and another chap on a bike had seen what had happened and he offered to escort me for a while to make sure I was OK. It was a beautiful evening and I really didn't want to miss out on my ride, so once I'd calmed down and stopped shaking, and my assailant had set off to break the news to her dad, I set off in the company of this chap. We'd been going for a while when I felt my phone vibrating in my pocket. I didn't bother to answer it because I was having too much of a nice time.

Then it rang again so I thought I better answer it. It was a message from my wife in a bit of a panic. A man had phoned and asked what had happened between, 'Your husband and my daughter'. It was the dad of the girl who had knocked me off. So I explained to her what had happened and told her I'd phone him when I got back.

When I did speak to him he proceeded to try to tell me it had all been my fault that his daughter had run into me, before realising that he was in the wrong and doing his best to assure me that , 'We'll say no more about it then'. I was livid – I couldn't believe he had the cheek to blame me, and then try to get me to promise I wouldn't be after him for some kind of compensation. If I hadn't felt so sorry for his daughter I'm sure I could have come up with some injury attributed to her inability to watch what she was doing, but in all honesty, I thought that if her dad always behaved like this, she'd probably suffered enough.

Fortunately I didn't have any injuries from which I needed to recover before I could get back to 'training' again, so my new regime could continue. I definitely started to feel the benefits – I was less breathless going up hills – by which I mean I could actually get up a hill without nearly being sick, and I began to notice clothes fitting me better again. I got to the stage where I could imagine myself wheeling effortlessly along the sea front at Scarborough at the end of my sponsored ride, being welcomed into the arms of my wife and children.

I hadn't, however, reached the status of someone who is truly in training. I knew this because I was always honest if someone asked me how often I went out on my bike. If anything, I tended to talk myself up a bit – rounding my numbers up rather than down. The rule amongst the truly dedicated is, of course, to deny that you train at all. Ask any top level club rider and they'll never admit to doing much, if any, training. In exactly the same way that the girl in school who always came top in every exam always said she never did any revision, cyclists all over the world deny that they ever do any serious training. Usually they'll admit to doing 'not much'. This is of course a very subjective definition. If I go out for a ride now and do fifteen miles, it's 'not much'. If I'd done that the first time I got back on my bike it would have been 'loads'. However, in the vast majority of cases, the 'not much' that most cyclists do involves cycling to work nearly every day, a couple of hard rides on midweek evenings, and a long one at the weekend. Not much at all if you say it fast.

The day of the charity ride finally came round. It seemed fitting that I was to be accompanied by Dicco. My brother was going to try out his new car by driving along the route with my children in the back so that they could stop at strategic points to cheer us on. I also hoped that they'd be able to come up alongside us from time to time to tell us how we were doing and to pass us drinks and bits of food through the car windows, just like they do for the professionals on the television. The weather was pretty lousy – grey and wet with a bit of a wind. We set off in a big group, but Dicco and I just went at our own pace, and found that true to form (we were the only proper cyclists, there after all), we left everyone behind. It was great to see the children waving to us when they went past in my brother's car, and from the roadside, and my dad got a photo of us going over the biggest hill of the day.

We got to the end in about four hours and walked up into town and, in the same way that professionals do, did our best to ingest plenty of protein and carbohydrate. In our case this meant we filled ourselves up on fish and chips before walking back to the finish line to see the others come in. No one had arrived so we set off back along the route and met everyone else just as they came into the outskirts of Scarborough.

It had been a fantastic day - my first 'event' since coming out of retirement. What I didn't realise at the time was that my obsession had become infectious, and I was about to get myself a new training partner, and that together we would set our sights higher than I had ever thought we would.

Stage 5
The Evangelist's First Convert

Arriving in Prague for a holiday, I was following a couple down the steps from the plane onto the tarmac. The woman looked around as we walked towards the terminal, and asked her husband if he knew why the wing tips of the plane were turned upwards. He gave a knowing look, and proceeded to explain that it was something to do with reducing turbulence. He expanded his answer by pointing out the subtle differences between each plane we could see parked on the tarmac, and how raised wing-tips had been developed. He was still in full flow at passport control, and was oblivious to the fact that his wife had long passed the point of boredom and looked as if she was considering sneaking off to get back on the plane home.

Many people become passionate about things that interest them, often to the point of seeming to be obsessed. You can tell by the way they come alive whenever conversation touches on their favourite subject, and just like the aeroplane obsessed man I had seen in Prague, these people can be both a pleasure and a pain to be with (I think plane man may well have been in the latter category). I'm sure I'm like this sometimes if I get onto the subject of cycling. I can talk about it for hours, usually without actually reaching any type of a conclusion. Whenever anyone asks me about riding a bike it's as if they have lit a blue touch paper, they should probably then retire to a safe distance. I tend to reassure myself by believing that I'm not as bad as someone who's just become a parent, or who has an unhealthy interest in aircraft wing tip design.

The more I cycled, the more I found to talk about, and one thing that had begun to fascinate me was an event I read about called the Etape du Tour. The closest translation of this is 'stage of the tour', or in this case 'stage of the Tour de France'. It is an event that is probably the cycling equivalent of the London Marathon – a day when several thousand cyclists get to ride a stage of the Tour de France. The route changes every year, just like the real thing, but the format is always the same. People from all over the world enter, and for one day in the year get to feel as close as they're ever going to as to how a top professional feels. All the roads are closed, there are motorcycle outriders just like those who support the professional race, and the people who live on the route decorate the streets and come out to cheer the riders on, lending a hand to the fulfilment of the dreams of thousands of middle aged men. Best of all, it follows the exact route that the real riders do. So once a mere mortal like you or I have ridden it, they can all go home and watch it on the television and say, truthfully, 'I did that'.

One person who had been on the bike ride to Scarborough was Nicky's husband – she was the mum from nursery who had been one of the first people I knew to view me as a 'proper' cyclist. Paul and I met a couple of times over the next few months, and he was one of the people who was often within earshot on one of the many occasions that I was rambling on about cycling. Somehow it must have stirred something in him and I realised just how much this had affected him one day when we were watching my wife and Nicky run the local version of the 'Race for Life'. We were standing against the ropes at the side of the road, squinting our eyes into the sun looking for our wives among the crowd of runners who ranged from trained athletes to those in fancy dress.

Paul had made the all too common mistake of asking me about cycling (he obviously didn't know any better at this point). I had, as ever, started droning on about how much I was enjoying it. I also told him about the Etape du Tour. I think my true motive for telling him this was to somehow make my interest more public.

I thought that if I told someone that I wanted to ride the Etape du Tour, this might make me do something other than just think about it. I worked on the basis that once you make an idea public you run the risk of making yourself looking stupid if you don't act on it. Paul looked thoughtful and stared into the sunset. 'Fuck it' he said. 'Fuck it – I'll fucking do it!'

This was the point at which I really couldn't back out – even though I fully intended to do the Etape, Paul's outburst meant that I no longer had a choice. If this non-cycling new friend of mine thought he could do the Etape, I should be able to do it, easily.

I still had no idea how to go about entering, so even though I had committed me and Paul to riding, I knew that if I couldn't find a way to enter I'd only, so far, left myself open to looking stupid to one person.

I had mentioned the idea of doing the Etape a few times to friends and family before, but I don't think anyone, myself included, ever thought anything would really come of it, but once I'd got talking to Paul about the idea, it seemed to grow and grow. He also told Carol, who had organised the charity ride we had done to Scarborough. I was now completely cornered. It was check mate to the detractors – there was absolutely no way I could drop out. The charity had been the reason behind the sponsored ride that we did to Scarborough and the day that had started Paul's interest in riding a bike. Carol thought it was a fantastic idea and decided that she too would like to ride. Things were really getting serious now and with more and more people learning of our plans, it made the whole thing much more real. There really was no way out – I had to find a way in and get our entry sorted. As the 'real cyclist' out of the three of us I thought I really should be the one to make sure that it happened.

At the time it was actually pretty difficult to get into the Etape if you lived outside France. It was also pretty difficult to get in if you lived *in* France. Its organised by the French national cycling publication, 'Velo' magazine. The entry form would come out in the February issue each year (there was no internet entry back then), and if you were lucky enough to live in France, get yourself to the local newsagent on the day the February issue came out, filled it in, got your medical certificate signed later that day, got to 'la poste' before lunch and sent off your entry, you *might* have had a chance of your entry being one of the ones that was accepted. Obviously, living in Yorkshire made that particular route impossible as it carried the added proviso that you need an address in France.

I suppose that this was a way of keeping this very French event as French as possible, after all, the Tour de France is hugely important in French life and culture, and as they haven't had a winner in over thirty years, there is an understandable reluctance to let foreigners take over the amateur version as well. In a way, the Tour has almost become like Britain in the football World Cup or in tennis at Wimbledon. Every year the press is full of expectation of how we might *finally* do it this year – only for it all to end in disappointment and a huge amount of blame and pressure being placed on individuals who in reality, are almost at the pinnacle of their sport. The difference being *almost* rather than *actually*. The French have become used to cheering on the honourable loser, like in 2004, the year a Frenchman, Thomas Voekler, held on to the lead in the Tour for almost two weeks, and became a national hero in the process, even though by the time the race ended in Paris he was well down the overall classification. He repeated this in 2012, this time managing to finish fourth overall and once again becoming hugely popular with the French public.

I looked on the internet for a way in – this looked much more hopeful as there was a wealth of travel companies who ran trips with guaranteed entries. The trouble was that there were so many sites it was a bit overwhelming so each time I looked things just seemed to get more confusing. I even asked one of my mum and dads friends if their daughter could sort me out by using the address of her holiday home, but that came to nothing too.

I was talking to Paul about these difficulties one day when he mentioned that he already knew someone who had done 'some kind of big bike ride in France'. He said he'd ask them if they had any advice that might help us find a way of getting an entry to the Etape. It turned out that this 'big bike ride in France' had actually been the Etape du Tour, so after a couple of phone calls we had our contact, and sent off all the paperwork. One evening in November, having spent most of my working day sneaking in and out of a meeting to send and receive faxes, I got an e-mail thanking me for my deposit, and confirming our place. That was it. We were in. Martin Gatenby was finally going to ride the Tour de France. Well, a bit of it anyway.

It was now a serious undertaking. Before long we were part of group that had grown to about seven people, so there was plenty of bravado, and endless talking about training, nutrition, physiological tuning and tactics for the day etc. This resulted in a finely tuned program of: eating and drinking a lot, riding our bikes as much as we could over the winter, then planning to pedal as fast and for as long as we could on the day. Lance Armstrong himself couldn't have come up with a better scheme. As part of my motivational plan, I printed a profile of the route and stuck it on our kitchen wall so I had to look at it every day. My diet continued to be the same old combination of carbohydrates, proteins and fluids (pasta, meat, beer, curry etc). As for physical conditioning, I once again heeded the best advice of the older members of the Hull Thursday Road Club when Dicco and I used to ask for training hints - 'Just ride your bloody bike son'.

Of course this gave me even more of an excuse to read up on all things cycling in an attempt to find the secret of success. The trouble is that as soon as you start to do this you are faced with the dawning realisation that you are not the finely tuned athlete you think yourself to be. You're a middle aged man who doesn't do enough exercise, has a terrible diet and drinks too much. The annoying thing was that I actually have a pretty healthy diet − I always eat my 'five a day', and although I love nothing more than good quality beer, I don't drink alcohol to excess. Having said that, I am at least a middle aged man who doesn't do enough exercise, has a terrible diet and drinks too much *but* I also have time for friends and family who still talk to me. Had I closely followed most of the advice I read I would have been a very lonely, hungry and unhappy man indeed. A lot of the advice in magazines and on the internet expected me to fit in ten hours of training and two decent length rides each weekend. They also advised against all but the smallest amounts of beer, pie and many other enjoyable things, although most of them admitted the occasional glass of red wine wouldn't damage my performance too much. Compared to the lifestyle advocated by some internet and magazine articles, monks have an easier time than someone trying to get fit for a long bike ride.

The following spring, Paul and I decided to do a regular ride every Sunday morning. The problem was that 'every Sunday' actually meant 'every Sunday when we can, and it isn't raining. Or freezing. Or blowing a gale. Or neither of us has a hangover.'

The other problem was that Paul didn't actually own a bike, which clearly put him at something of a disadvantage. In what I liked to think of as good timing, I got an unexpected bonus at work, so I decided that I'd do both Paul and myself a big favour by spending it on a new bike, and thus freeing up my old bike, which I could sell to Paul. Of course, Paul, as a new cyclist, didn't only need a bike, but all the additional bits of kit – helmet, shorts, shoes and anything else that I could convince him he couldn't be without. I always enjoy a bit of time spending money in bike shops, so we spent a happy couple of hours in a local shop getting him kitted out. I was only there to remind him of what he needed, but I think he also didn't want to be convinced by an over eager salesman that he couldn't possibly start to ride a bike seriously without having the latest type of carbon fibre screw driver (or be told that he was far too old to be cycling anyway). The only time Paul really raised his eyebrows (apart from paying), was when the chap in the shop was advising him about the need for cream to rub on your behind before a long ride. He left the shop seeming happy with what he had bought; meaning the only thing left to do was for us to get fit.

Luckily, there are plenty of hills around where we live. In the early stage of our 'training' (for that is what our rides had now become), this seemed to be a bad thing. There seemed to be no way of leaving home without quickly finding yourself heading uphill. The organizers of the Etape like your day as a professional cyclist to be as special as possible, and always try to use one of the mountain stages of the race, so hilly terrain was just what we needed. This means that entrants can get excited about being able to ride some of the most iconic roads in the world of cycling. Of course, it is easy to forget that the very reason that makes these roads so iconic is exactly the same reason you shouldn't ride them unless you have to - they are incredibly tough. I remember watching riders struggling up the great mountains of the Tour, and wanting to do exactly the same thing myself. There are endless famous film clips of heroic acts of suffering by some of history's greatest riders. They are very inspiring, but had I thought about the scenes shown in those clips a little more objectively, I would have realised that if a highly gifted and well trained athlete is going to be driven to needing oxygen at the top of a mountain (like Steven Roche did at the top the la Plagne climb in 1987), then an average cyclist was going to be at risk of being reduced to tears (as Martin Gatenby was on the Col de Port de Bales in 2007), or worse still doing themselves some lasting harm.

Paul and I took advantage of our local environment by riding out onto the moors in search of some hills. There is no shortage of steep hills around Yorkshire. They differ from the climbs in France because although they're very steep, they are rarely of the leg sapping length of anything in Europe.

'Are we going over there?' asked Paul one day when we were on the moors looking for another piece of road that would cause us to almost turn blue with the effort taken to ride up it. He was pointing at the horizon – a great grey mass against a pale sky.

'Over where?' I asked.

'That hill'.

'That's not a hill, it's a cloud'.

'Bollocks, it's a hill'.

'Well it must be a new one then, because it wasn't there this time last week'.

This was quite typical of the type of discussion Paul and I fell into when we were out on our bikes. I think our respective wives thought that we spent the long hours on rides putting the world to rights, but in reality we had the same type of discussions that most men generally have when they're in each other's company – moaning about work, talking about work, the usual 'manly' stuff. On this occasion we happened to be arguing about whether the horizon was formed by a big hill, or a big cloud. This might sound strange, but on a grey day, if the sun shines a certain way, clouds can look like hills, and hills like clouds. But on this occasion, I was right and Paul was wrong.

A few months later we were on our way to Pau for the Etape. Paul was dozing in the passenger seat when I woke him. We were approaching a motorway toll and he needed to pay, partly because the toll booth was on his side, and partly because we were using his credit card to pay for everything.

It was a beautiful summer's evening. The sky was a deep blue and there were hardly any clouds. I looked to the West, at the dark shapes of the horizon climbing upwards.

'Looks a bit cloudy over there', I said.

'That's not clouds its mountains', Paul said.

We'd been here before – the same old optical illusion. Carol was in the seat between us, but couldn't seem to settle the argument, and then Paul pointed out that clouds don't usually have snow on top. He was right – they were mountains and not clouds. Their dark shape seemed to climb impossibly high into the sky, moving the horizon much further up than it should have been. We realised that these were the Pyrenees – and that in a couple of days' time we'd be trying to ride over them. Just to dispel any doubts about this, we pulled in at the next lay-by, and found ourselves underneath a stainless steel sculpture depicting 'Le Tour de France dans le Pyrenees'.

Although we felt that the hundreds of miles that we'd ridden around the Yorkshire Dales was good preparation for the Etape, the scale of the mountains in Europe is totally different. When you climb up a hill in England and want to see how far it is to the top, you usually just need to raise your eyebrows, but to see the top of a French mountain, you have to look up so far that it hurts your neck. I remember looking for the top of the Col d'Aubisque, and seeing a village clinging onto the mountainside. It looked like it was hanging from a thread way above my left shoulder. The thing was, it wasn't at the top. It wasn't even *near* the top.

Like many mountains, the Col d'Aubisque has a cruel trick to play as you near the summit. You approach a road-side hotel that is on the crest of a rise in the road. On the day we did it there was quite a crowd watching us. It looks like the top, but as you use the last bit of energy that you feel you can possibly muster, you look to your right and see the road zigzagging even higher. Luckily I'd read about this beforehand so I was expecting it, if it had taken me by surprise I'm sure I'd have been devastated and wanted to give up there and then.

One thing we had no chance of preparing ourselves for was the heat, although a friend did suggest putting on as many clothes as possible and pedalling away on a stationary bike indoors to give us some idea of what to expect. Michael Hutchinson, the multiple time trial champion, did this in preparation for his attempt on the world hour record. Paul and I decided between us that as there were no world records at stake for us, we'd just take a chance on being able to cope on the day.

Most of our training seemed to take place in foul weather. The romantic image of cycling that I tend to hold in my head is of a glorious summers evening, out on the moors for a couple of hours, perhaps with a nice pint outside a pub on the way home. The reality of the hours we put in was that it always seemed to rain. There was one summer's day when we had set off on part of the route of a local challenge ride called the 'Etape du Dales' (best said in a Yorkshire accent). We had only done about six miles when Paul had a puncture. By the time we had sorted it out I was suggesting that maybe we should call it a day because it was starting to rain heavily. 'It'll brighten up soon', Paul said, so we set off to climb over the moors, before our route dropped down a steep hill into the famous cheese making town of Hawes. It was raining so much that there were great rivers of water running off the moors and across our path, washing stones, grass and leaves into the road. We finally got into to the town centre and huddled under a shop awning. I was totally fed up and well on my way to concluding that cycling was a stupid sport for stupid people who should probably find something better to do, such as spending Saturday afternoons in the pub reading a newspaper, warm and cosy and letting the world pass by outside.

'We'll go over Buttertubs now' said Paul. 'Buttertubs' is another high moor that lies in the direction of Cumbria and on this day was totally obscured by a thick mist.

'No', I replied.

'Come on', said Paul, 'It won't be too bad'.

'Fuck off', I said, 'there is no fucking way I'm going over Butter tubs today'. I was beginning to lose my temper, but Paul clearly didn't realise, or didn't care.

'It'll be fine', he said.

'Bollocks it will be fine. I'm fucking soaked and I'm freezing.'

'I'll run you a bath', offered Paul.

'What?'

'A bath, I've never offered to run anyone a bath in my life. I think you should go for it'.

'I don't care if you rub my fucking back, I'm not doing it'.

There were one or two people beginning to eves drop on us, and I was beginning to run out of expletives. I realised that the sight of two grown men, dressed in skin tight Lycra, and arguing about an offer of a bath and a back rub might seem a bit out of place in a market town in the Yorkshire Dales, so I got my map out and, after a few seconds of careful study, worked out that we could take a huge short cut. It meant we could still take a fairly rounded way back, so Paul compromised and we set off on our slightly shorter route. It was still up a huge, long hill, head long into wind and rain and probably every bit as unpleasant as going over Buttertubs would have been but at least I felt to have got my own way.

Paul's enthusiasm for training always seemed to put me to shame. He was always keener to go out than me. If it looked like it might rain, I would often make excuses and stay at home. I'd look at the weather and almost feel relieved when it started raining, thus justifying my decision to stay in bed. Paul worked on the theory that by denying the weather forecast, it would somehow mean that the inevitable rain wouldn't affect him. He constantly seemed to demonstrate an ability to deny the laws of physics, but then express total, genuine, surprise when he was proved wrong.

He once phoned me at about half past three on a winter afternoon. I pointed out that we wouldn't really have time for a ride because it would be getting dark in the next hour or so. Undeterred by this, Paul set out alone. He told me later that he'd had a really terrible ride because he'd had to walk home along the grass verge because it had 'suddenly' got dark. I found out from his wife about one occasion on a hot day when he got home and found he was locked out. Thirsty from his ride, he drank tepid water from his garden hose. He only admitted this to Nicky twenty four hours later when he got a 'mystery' tummy upset.

There was a slow realisation from the two of us over those months that we were gradually turning into 'proper' cyclists. Paul had befriended the proprietor of one of the local bike shops, and we began to develop the ability to carry on a conversation as we rode over hills that used to leave us gasping for breath, and we began to wonder if we were doing enough 'training'. We didn't resort to shaving our legs, but we both drank a bit less beer, and ate a slightly better diet.

I'd met someone who thought I was a proper cyclist, and since meeting him, we'd both learned a lot about ourselves, and a bit about how to ride a bike a few miles. Now when *he* met people, they thought *he* was a proper cyclist too.

Stage 6
Learning Curve

As Paul and I started to ride our bikes more and more, with a big event to focus on, there was a new element to contend with – pressure, albeit a very low level of pressure, which was entirely self-inflicted. This wasn't about how fit we were, or whether or not we were riding to our full potential, but once we were committed to riding a whole stage of the Tour de France, simply mucking about on our bikes as a way of keeping healthy was no longer enough.

I had started out riding my bike for pleasure, supposedly free of the worry of needing to train for races, but I was quickly starting to find that I was worrying about how much riding I should have been doing. I seemed to forget that I was supposed to be doing it for fun. I had already become accustomed to suffering in order to get fit at my twice weekly spinning classes, and although these sessions were becoming less painful, they were still a long way from being a pleasure. Admittedly, there is very little pleasure in a spin class, no matter how fit you are, and I had reached the conclusion that if anyone reaches a point where spin classes are their idea of a good night out, then they might have room for a little reassessment of their life.

I persuaded myself that the evenings spent working so hard at these classes at least meant that my Sunday morning rides would be easier and therefore much more fun. Unfortunately, I had reached the point where I began to see these so called pleasure rides as another opportunity to make myself suffer. Every time I set out, I'd fully intend to enjoy the ride, take in the scenery and not over-do things. In reality, what happened as soon as I was out of town and onto the quieter country roads, a red mist would descend, and I'd push myself as hard as I could for as long as I could, before reminding myself that there was no need for me to be doing this. After all, I was getting ready to go to France for a pleasure ride. I had somehow crossed a line between 'pleasure rides' and 'training rides', but this had obviously happened without me realising it.

One of my motivational tricks in the run up to the first Etape that Paul and I had entered was to put a profile of the route up in the kitchen so that I saw it every day. This filled me with a child-like excitement every time I saw it and thought of finally riding a stage of the Tour de France, but frightened me just about as much every time someone else commented on how hard it looked. When one friend saw it he asked, 'So how long will it take you to do?'

'Hopefully less than nine hours', was my confident answer. He'd put me on the spot a bit, so I'd come to this figure by the simple scientific process of making a rough guess.

'Bloody hell, I thought you were going to say a week!' he replied.

It dawned on me that this 'pleasure' ride was actually a serious undertaking and that there was a real chance that Paul and I might not finish. No matter how many times I traced my finger along the route profile on the kitchen wall, it didn't start to look any easier.

The problem was that although it was apparent that entering and completing the Etape was a pretty serious challenge, I wasn't clear in my own mind exactly how serious I should become about it. I knew I'd have to ride my bike more, but it didn't stop there; there were endless lifestyle changes I could make in the pursuit of better performance, but as the cost to my happiness of many of these things would be considerable, and the benefits impossible to measure, I wanted to stick to simply doing more exercise, working on the old theory of achieving a life-style balance by training hard, and eating and drinking just as I did before.

I decided a bit of research might help. Since my 'comeback' to the world of cycling I had become an avid reader of all the regular cycling publications. These would often contain training advice and tips from all sorts of sources – ex-professionals, regular club riders and the new breed of 'fitness coaches', all of whom had plenty to say. Most of it made me feel inadequate, and left me overwhelmed and puzzled as to the best things to do.

One ex-professional advocated riding with bricks in your saddle bag, obviously working on the theory that the extra load would make your rides more beneficial because of the extra weight you had to haul around. As saddle bags went out of fashion at about the time this chap hung up his wheels, I realised that this particular course of action wasn't open to me.

Riding up hills non-handed seemed to offer more promise. After all, I'd need to improve my climbing if I was going to get all the way around the mountains that would make up the Etape course, so here was a chance to work on an aspect of my fitness that would really be of benefit on the day. The idea is that you are forced make more use of your leg muscles, rather than pulling on the handlebars with your arms to gain a bit of extra leverage. I quickly realised that the major flaw in this particular plan was that you need to be going at a reasonable speed to keep your balance whilst riding non-handed, and I couldn't keep moving quickly enough up hill to safely take my hands off the bars.

I came across other suggestions too but dismissed most of them out of hand, especially the idea of holding your breath for as long as possible whilst riding, because the article in which I read about this particular piece of thinking pointed out that the only person who had tried it was dead.

The turbo trainer was another invention that had come along in the years whilst I wasn't cycling. This is a home training (or home torture) device designed to have a bike bolted to it. You can then pedal away for as long as you like, without having to worry about the weather, the dark nights or getting home later than planned. So if I had a turbo, I couldn't use the weather, dark nights or the chance of getting home later than planned as a reason not to get some training done. A lot of the things I had read in all those magazines seemed to think that turbo trainers were a good thing, so naturally I went out and bought one. This meant that not only could I obsessively read about all the things I should be doing whilst out on the road on my bike, but I could now uncover a whole new world of training ideas, and ways of measuring the fact that I was nowhere near as fit as most other cyclists. All of this was made possible without me actually having to leave the house.

One of the great disadvantages of the turbo trainer is that once I had got my cycling kit on, got a towel to mop up all my sweat, turned on a big desk fan to cool myself down, then sat there pedalling away, it took me less than five minutes to be bored out of my mind. As I have always been a bit of a music fan my first solution to this problem was to make up a few CDs to pedal along to. I revisited my youth with a bit of AC/DC, The Clash, various old punk compilations, and a few slow songs thrown in, which I included to allow me to have a rest, or slow down my pedalling speed and pretend I was going uphill. I also got hold of a few dance albums which were at least similar to many of the ones I had got used to at my spin classes for a bit of high speed pedalling along to the pounding bass beat. I even started enjoying them for their musical content after a while. In addition to all this, I could even simulate the riding uphill non-handed training method, because the bike was securely bolted to the floor, so even if my theoretical speed was very low, I could stay upright.

Inevitably, there's only so much boredom that can be overcome by pretending to ride uphill non-handed, and by listening to old albums, no matter how much they might make you want to pedal faster. I had noticed in the instruction book for my turbo trainer that there were a couple of suggested sessions to do. The book described how 'exercising more, quitting smoking, and healthy eating' were the 'new way of life'. They probably should have added 'trying to re-live dreams of your childhood on a bike', which I think would have been more appealing. Add to this the benefits of sitting in your spare bedroom with your bike bolted to a turbo trainer and cycling greatness, and possibly eternal life, seemed all but guaranteed. The sessions had names like 'hill training' (just what I needed), 'Power training' (not sure if I needed that one) and 'Recovery' (definitely needed). I carefully copied them out, and printed them in a font large enough to be read through eyes filled with sweat, and found that I had discovered another way of alleviating the boredom of the turbo trainer. I didn't mind the sessions at first, and once I'd expanded my collection of sessions with a few examples that I downloaded from the internet, I developed quite a varied routine. Combining old rock albums and new turbo sessions gave an almost infinite variety of combinations. I began to wonder how I ever found sessions on the turbo boring.

Despite the fact that I was starting to feel the benefits of all my extra training, I still continued my quest to find the golden bullet that would transform me into a world class cyclist. My next discovery was that simply pushing myself to the point of exhaustion wasn't enough, even if I was pushing myself to the point of exhaustion in a fairly structured way. What I found was that in order for this to work effectively, I had to measure how exhausted I was by using a heart rate monitor. It was something of a surprise to discover that these little machines had a use outside the walls of a hospital, and I found the talk of 'twenty minutes in zone two' and 'three times five minutes at threshold' mystifying and confusing. Even so, I knew that if I was to take the next step towards my goal, I would have to have a heart rate monitor.

Chemist shops no longer seem to stock the little bottles of olive oil, and strange tasting sweets that they did when I was a boy, although they do stock numerous gadgets aimed at convincing perfectly healthy but gullible members of the public that they need to keep a closer eye on every aspect of their physical well-being. They are probably creating quite a good market amongst slightly obsessive middle aged men who have just started exercising again, and it was whilst I was in a chemist shop that I saw a heart rate monitor for sale for the very reasonable price of ten pounds. I bought it immediately and couldn't wait to get it home so I could analyse my new training regime in a previously unimagined level of detail.

The problem with a lot of modern technology is summed up by the phrase 'rubbish in equals rubbish out'. I realised that I could read and record as much information from my heart rate monitor as I wanted, but unless I knew what all this information was supposed to mean, I wasn't going to benefit from it. I learned that the 'zones' I read about were all related to my maximum heart rate, which I could easily work out by subtracting my age from 220. Or by pedalling for ten minutes at a rate at which I could easily hold a conversation (which would obviously involve me sitting on a static bike and talking to myself, which would probably look a bit strange if anyone saw me), then looking at my heart rate on my shiny new heart rate monitor and doubling whatever it said. Once this was done I could easily converse about what zone I was in, and for how long. At first, I don't think that all this knowledge was of much use, but at least it gave me something else to concentrate on whilst pedalling away on my turbo. This added another layer of variety to such an extent that the turbo was almost becoming interesting.

As I got used to having a heart rate monitor, I eventually began to see its potential, by just using it in the same way as a rev counter on a car. If it showed my heart rate was high for a long time, I'd ease off for a while, knowing that I could let my heart rate go up if the terrain got really hard. It certainly helped me on longer rides to pace myself, but I never relied on it as much as one top level racer I read about who blamed a disappointing result on his heart rate monitor (rather than his actual heart) when it stopped working.

Having read everything I could find about training methods, heart rates, turbo sessions and spin classes, I realised that there was a whole new world of things to worry about if I started to look at my diet. So far I hadn't really changed my eating habits, apart from my pre-ride breakfast. This always consisted of a big bowl of porridge and two scrambled eggs on toast. I'd only come up with this combination after reading that it was what pro-cyclist Roger Hammond did, and by my experience on my first long ride when the two jam sandwiches I'd taken with me hadn't been enough to give me the energy I needed. I'd also read that a strong espresso before setting out was a good way of making my body burn fat, so I started doing that as well.

Of course, it was easy enough for me to get plenty to eat before setting out, but keeping myself fed whilst out on my bike was another challenge. The Etape would mean almost a whole day on my bike, a hearty breakfast wasn't going to keep me going through to the finish, so I needed to find a way of avoiding what is known in the cycling world as 'bonking'. This is when the body has used up all its energy reserves and your blood sugar levels fall so low that you feel too weak to carry on. The effects can be dramatic – riders becoming unable to turn the pedals, and in its most extreme cases becoming disorientated, even collapsing. When Dicco and I used to go out all day, we carried our 'bonk bags' on our backs, filled with things like golden syrup sandwiches and chocolate biscuits. These bags have gone out of fashion now, apart from their use in professional races when team helpers hand them to the riders who transfer their contents to their jersey pockets, before throwing the bag to a grateful spectator.

I found that Golden Syrup sandwiches had gone out of fashion too, and a whole new industry of 'sports nutrition' had sprung up during my years off the bike. This meant that sandwiches had been replaced by energy bars and sachets of gel. I got a free energy bar on the front of a magazine, and used it on another longer ride. I'd seen the professionals get these from their pockets and tuck into them without even a pause in their pedalling. What I didn't know was that those helpers who passed their energy bars to them had taken the trouble to cut the package open so that the rider could actually get to the bar and eat it. I found that the wrappers on these bars were so difficult to open that by the time I'd tugged at it with my teeth, sworn at it, nearly lost my balance as I tore the packaging, then finally managed to get it at least partly open, the energy bar inside was mashed to a pulp before I could get any of it into my mouth. I also learned quite quickly that I needed to be on a fairly flat bit of road if I was going to eat whilst on the move, because as soon as I needed to make any effort, I needed my mouth to breath, not to eat. On one of the first occasions that I managed to get an energy bar out in one piece, I hardly got to eat any of it because it fell from my fingers into the side of the road, where it picked up a thick coating of grit. It was still there when I rode past again two weeks later – even the local crows had found it too difficult to deal with.

The gels presented a slightly different set of challenges. They are at least designed to be opened with your teeth, so access wasn't a problem, but controlling the sticky slop as it squirted out of the sachet was another art form I had to master. I became used to my hands and face becoming as sticky as fly-paper, and as attractive to flies as well.

There was much debate amongst the ever growing number of people I rode with about what was the ideal food for aspiring cyclists, especially what to eat whilst actually out on our bikes. I don't think any of us were so dedicated that our entire dietary input was going to become so carefully controlled that we'd be measuring every portion of every single thing that we'd eat, but many of us had our own particular favourites. As most of the energy bars I had bought seemed to vaguely resemble flapjack, I decided to save a bit of money by making flapjack at home, often only to find that when I went to get some ready for an early Sunday morning ride, that the tin was empty, and my children would be asking when I was going to make another batch.

Nigel, a mountain biker whose interest in road biking led him to come out with us from time to time had a taste for pork pies. Although most sports nutritionists would baulk at the thought of a pork pie, they do contain plenty of the salts sweated away by a cyclist, some fat to lubricate the joints, protein to rebuild tired muscles and come self-contained in their own edible carbohydrate packaging. They are not, however, widely available in France, so any pork pie nutrition for the Etape would have to be taken with us. I can't begin to imagine what sort of state a pork pie would be in having being transported from home to the South of France, so it lost its place on our menu for the big day.

Paul's favourite solution was the Mars bar. Again, this has a lot going for it, as it's tasty and provides just the sort of sugar boost that makes you feel better on a long ride. The problem is that even on a cool day, your body heat can pass through your jersey pockets to enough of an extent to melt a Mars Bar, and so in the heat of a French afternoon in mid-July, they'd be no good at all. Undeterred, Paul decided that he'd at least get his Mars bar fix for the first part of the day by putting his Mars Bars in the freezer of our hotel room and eating them as they defrosted in his pocket.

So, despite all our 'trials', and hours of discussing the merits of the great Mars Bar versus Pork Pie versus Flapjack debate, Paul and I stocked up on energy bars and gels. The day before our first Etape we spent a couple of hours wandering around the trade stands in the start village, when we started to worry that we didn't have enough gels, bars and sachets of high energy, caffeine loaded drinks, and spent a small fortune on doubling our supplies. By the time I had combined my new purchases with those that I had brought from home, I had supplies enough to have a bar about every ten minutes, with a gel to wash it down in between. I could easily have consumed enough calories to have put weight on despite all the efforts of the ride. All I had to do was to remember to eat regularly throughout the day, which, even after all my research, might seem easy, but the motto 'eat before you're hungry, drink before you're thirsty', is a surprisingly easy thing to forget.

Even though I don't ever remember changing my every day diet, the natural consequence of all the exercise I was doing meant that I found I could eat as much as I wanted without gaining any weight, and I started to notice that clothes fitted me better. I lost count of the times that people would look at my plate of food and make comments like, 'You're lucky – you can eat all that and you're still thin'. I had to agree that I did often think that I was lucky to be able to eat a lot and not put on any weight, although I did point out to these people that I usually thought this half way through yet another spin class or turbo session, or towards the end of another hundred kilometre bike ride. It was a bit like when golfer Gary Player sank a thirty foot putt, and as he walked away, a woman in the crowd said, 'That was lucky Mr Player'. He turned and said, 'Its funny, the more I practice, the luckier I seem to get'.

It was the same with me. With everything I'd learned, and all the time I spent pedalling away, either at home or out on the road, the more I practiced, the luckier I seemed to get. The truth is that I am lucky, lucky that I love a pastime that has the fortunate side effect of being good for me. If I'd fallen in love with darts instead of cycling, and tried to emulate the darts heroes of the nineteen seventies, instead of the cycling heroes, I'd probably weigh a fair bit more than I do now, and be trying yet again to give up smoking.

Eventually of course, every run of good luck comes to an end. As Paul and I got 'luckier' (or possibly just fitter), we found ourselves being able to catch up with other groups of cyclists, and ride along with them without too much difficulty. We'd occasionally surprise ourselves by being able to cruise past other people, nodding a nonchalant 'Hello' as we breezed by. At other times of course, things worked the other way and we'd be caught and passed by fitter and faster riders.

One sunny Sunday in autumn, we were riding along at what we thought was a fairly quick, but still comfortable speed when we heard a voice from behind us say, 'Morning lads'. Dressed as we were in all our best cycling gear, we turned around expecting to see someone looking like a professional, slightly out of breath as a result of the effort taken to catch up with us. It wouldn't be unfair to say that the man who had greeted us didn't look like a cyclist. He was on a racing bike, but instead of wearing the usual Lycra cycling kit he was dressed in an anorak, a woolly jumper, jeans and Wellington boots. I couldn't believe it. What made it worse was that he wasn't having any trouble keeping up with us. I was used to the occasional cocky teenager on a mountain bike catching us before being left behind, out of breath, but this chap didn't even look to be trying. He apologised for his appearance (which could best be described as 'covered in shit') by explaining that he was a dairy farmer and had nipped out for a ride after doing the morning milking. I was starting to wonder if all the improvements I had made were a figment of my imagination when I could be caught so easily by someone who was cycling in wellies. Luckily, after chatting for a while, our new riding partner told us that he was a fell runner using cycling as a way of getting ready for the national championships, where he had a decent chance of getting into the top ten. This made me feel a bit better. Maybe I *was* actually a lot fitter than I used to be. Maybe I *had* learned something.

With all this new found knowledge, and even the chance to share it occasionally, I had begun to feel like I might actually know what I was doing. I was no longer blindly feeling my way through a mid-life crisis. I had learned secret training methods, began to understand the physiology of an athlete, and knew how to keep my newly found athlete's body in tune through correct nutrition. I could ride up hills non-handed, nod knowingly about 'twenty minutes in zone two', and even knew how long it took me to work off the calories contained in a Pork Pie.

Stage 7
The New Golf

I've never been any good at ball sports. This obviously benefited me when my dad wrote to Mr DeVries and got me out of PE lessons so I could ride my bike, but in many ways, my total inability to kick, throw, or hit a ball in anything resembling the right direction has been more of a hindrance than a help.

When I started a job in sales, a few people said to me that golf would be a good pastime to take up. After all, they said, it's on the golf course where you develop relationships and strike those all-important deals. However, even the opportunity for a bit of career progression didn't really leave me feeling as if I needed to try and overcome a lifetime of incompetence.

It was at a friend's wedding that I had my first try on a golf course. The groom, Les, wanted to spend the morning of his wedding day playing golf with a couple of the guests. It was only a small wedding and was held on Gigha, a beautiful island, just off the Mull of Kintyre.

Les wasn't a golfer either – he just thought it seemed a good idea. The course on Gigha is free of all the usual rules of most golf clubs, which often seem to be designed to dissuade anyone from wanting to play. This meant we could arrive at the club house – a six by eight foot garden shed with an honesty box and a small sign welcoming all players and wishing them a pleasant day, in casual shorts and t-shirts.

Four of us set out for the first tee, on a stunning sunny morning. Les seemed relaxed and happy, looking forward to seeing his plans for his perfect day coming together. The only regular golfer in our group, and the only owner of a set of clubs, was Mark. The other half of the foursome consisted of me and Jimmy, who were both beginning to regret trying to work our way down the entire Malt Whisky list in the bar the night before. The course gave us amazing views of almost the whole of the island, which is only about six miles long, and a couple of miles wide. As we got ourselves ready, we decided that as Mark owned the clubs, he should be given the honour of taking the first shot of the day. Les, Jimmy, and I looked on, impressed by his stance and the way he seemed to be able to hold the club so naturally.

We held our breath as Mark swung his club, and waited for the 'ping' of the metal club head striking the ball and sending it off into the distance. Unfortunately there was no 'ping' and the ball toppled off the tee and dribbled about six feet, before rolling down a little hill. Wiping the tears of laughter from our eyes, we decided to accept Mark's excuse that, 'It was just a practice' and let him have another go. After a few attempts he did manage to get the ball some distance towards the flag which we could just see in the middle of a far-off green. About twenty shots, and much laughter later, the four of us had finally finished the first hole. I would like to say that five shots each is not a bad effort for three beginners and one regular player, but those twenty shots were *shots each*, not shots between us. Somehow it was decided that I had been the least hopeless, so I should have the honour of taking the first shot on the second hole.

There was a little sign telling us that as this was only a short hole, we were expected to complete it in three shots. The real challenge was that the green sat at the bottom of a steep hill covered in heather, so it was quite likely that we were going to lose a few balls before we were done.

I grabbed a club (choosing the one with the biggest head), put the ball on its tee then swung as hard as I could. There was a sweet 'ping' and the four of us watched, utterly flabbergasted, as my ball arched into to sky before plopping onto the green and coming to a stop about six feet from the hole. I then had quite a long wait whilst the other three spent about twenty minutes trying to replicate what I'd done, and another twenty looking for lost balls in all the heather, before deciding that we'd better hurry up as it was only a few hours before we were due in church.

To say that I played well that day would be a total lie, as my 'beginners luck' started to fade after about six holes, but when we got back to the pub I amazed my wife by being able to tell her that I'd won. She was only slightly less incredulous than I was. I began to wonder if I had finally found a ball sport that suited me.

Inspired by my experience, I did actually buy a cheap set of clubs, and played a few times, but I began to realise that golf wasn't for me – once again the ball sport that suits me has yet to be created, and as its unlikely to involve bikes, I'm really not too bothered. I have nothing against people who play golf, in fact some of my best friends play the game, but I think the incident that finally confirmed my long held belief that golf is a perfectly pleasant game that I don't want to play, was the day I went to a local club to see if they had a driving range. I had been given directions by the man in the shop and was just driving out of the car park when two men ran over to my car and started banging on the windows. I assumed that I must have clipped one of the other cars in the car park, or, judging by their sense of panic, mown down a bus queue of pensioners, so I wound down my window to see what the problem was. They told me that I had had the cheek to drive the wrong way around the car park. Bearing in mind that the car park was virtually empty, it did seem something of an over-reaction. I dread to think what would have happened if I'd been wearing the wrong type of shoes at the time.

A couple of years later, following the re-awakening of my love of cycling, I was delighted to hear that the Tour de France would be holding its 2007 'Grand Depart' in London. This would give me the chance to realise another long held ambition and go and see the race in the flesh. The 'Grand Depart' is the carnival that takes place on the first day of the tour each year, and usually takes the form of a time trial around the land marks of the city chosen to play host. On the train journey on the way down to London, the newspapers were full of stories about cycling and about the tour. One writer described how cycling had become 'The new Golf'.

'New' would certainly be appropriate, as there has been a long history of cycling being seen as a 'working man's' sport. This might have something to do with the Clarion Cycling movement that began in late nineteenth century England. This was an organisation started by working class men in the Midlands who had found that cycling gave them a freedom that they hadn't been able to experience before. They wanted to set up an organisation that promoted 'the pleasures of cycling and the propaganda of Socialism'. It quickly grew to a group with over six thousand members, and rides would be organised that culminated in group meetings where riders would hear speeches about the Socialist perspective on affairs of the day.

There are many stories of the great riders of the fifties and sixties coming from tough backgrounds, and seeing cycling as a way out of poverty. Jacques Anquetil, the first man to win the Tour de France five times, came from a poor background, Tommy Simpson was the son of a miner, and Jean Stablinksi, Tommy's long term team mate, *was* a miner before he became a professional cyclist. As he raced across the cobbles of Belgium and Northern France in races like the Paris Roubaix and the Tour of Flanders, he said that he was the only man to have, 'suffered by racing over the cobbles and suffered by digging coal from under them'.

Golf has a long tradition that is in stark contrast to miners clawing their way to the top and finding fame and fortune. As a result of the fact that it takes quite a lot of money, a lot of time, and a lot of talent to be successful, it has, for many years created its own elite. The nature of the game is fairly sociable, and it has over time lent itself to the making of many business deals, and strong business relationships. It would never suit me however, because following my dreadful car park *faux pas* I had realised that it wasn't just my lack of skill that would be keeping me out of the club house.

Golfers will talk about their handicaps and how they 'hit a brilliant drive straight down the fairway on the fourth'. Cyclists will talk about how they 'got up Norwood Edge in the twenty three and kept my heart rate in zone three'. The one thing that golf does share with cycling however is that normally sensible men can spend lots of money in shops on shiny new toys that they can then talk to all their friends about for hours on end. They then get to spend many hours playing with these toys with the same friends whilst dressed in terrible clothes. Thought about in these terms, it is easy to see how cycling has become 'the new golf', as both activities allow badly dressed men to gather in large groups and talk about their tackle.

When Dicco and I used to pedal our way around East Yorkshire in the late nineteen seventies, we rarely came across other cyclists. These days, if Paul and I go out for a few hours on a Sunday morning, or I'm out on a club run, we'll usually see at least fifty other people like us, out cycling for the day. They all seem to be about our age and from talking to them, most seem to be relatively new to cycling (that is to say, they didn't cycle as youngsters, like Dicco and I did). There certainly seem to be plenty of middle-aged middle-class men who've turned down checked trousers and Pringle sweaters in favour of Lycra and wrap around shades. The cycling business has gone through something of a boom in recent years, with a ready market of men and women ready to part with their cash.

Having done all I could to eat better and train more, and to generally try to treat my body like that of a true athlete, the only thing left to worry about was equipment. I had decided that I needed something a bit better than my bike from Halfords (not that there was anything wrong with it, but I wasn't going to admit that), so started the process of getting myself another new bike, although this time, I had a bit more idea of what I was looking for.

Carlton Cycles, the company who had made the bikes that Dicco and I had ridden all those years ago had long since disappeared. It was swallowed up by the Raleigh Group in the late seventies and, in their wisdom, had been closed because it was seen as a part of the company that was 'diluting the brand'.

Back in those days most bikes were made of steel, which meant that the process of actually building a frame could be learned by anyone with the skill, patience and desire to become a bike builder. This led to a whole industry of independent bike shops who built their own brand of frames. They could be made to measure and always carried the name of the builder along their tubes. In my memory, these types of bikes were nearly always a dark colour, and carried names like 'Ted Scrimshaw' or 'Terry Bates' and the shops where they were manufactured had a kind of musty smell that must have been a combination of burnt welding materials, old tyres and woodbines. The advent of carbon fibre and the ability to mass produce aluminium frames in the Far East has led to these artisan frame builders all but dying out. So my search for a new bike would mean getting something mass produced.

I spent many happy hours surfing the internet, and began to try and put together a virtual version of my dream bike. There were so many to choose from that I felt a bit like a small child who'd been let loose in the world's biggest toy shop. I needed a reason to choose one out of the many and once again, my mind wandered back to my youth, and all the bikes Dicco and I used to drool over. One bike builder whose name was firmly lodged in my mind was that of Ernesto Colnago, an Italian who has been building bikes since the nineteen fifties. I remember those bikes being so far out of our reach that it would be a bit like looking at a Ferrari catalogue when I was thinking of buying myself a new car (something that is way out of reach at this time in my life). I had set myself a budget for my dream bike, and it didn't run to a Colnago. I could probably have scraped the money together, but didn't think it reasonable to expect my three children to go without food or clothes for six months just so I could ride about on a bike that was, in reality, far better than I deserved. I had just about settled on a slightly cheaper Italian (I knew it had to be Italian) bike when once again Dicco intervened.

This intervention came in the form of a text message that simply said, 'Mate selling c40 your size'. I phoned him straight away and he told me more about it. It was just a frame – no wheels or any bits that would make it function as a bike, but the chap selling it only wanted the same as I had already budgeted for during those hours spent putting my dream bike together on the internet. And most important of all, the name written along its tubes didn't sound like someone from a Dickens novel – it simply read 'Colnago'. It was just too good a chance to miss, so I bought it.

When I got it home my family were totally under-whelmed by what looked to them like something that was only any good for hanging clothes on. (Something that my middle son took to doing, much to his own amusement). I was delighted, and kept it proudly on my desk, leaning gently against the wall. I polished it regularly and I couldn't wait until I'd saved up enough to buy the parts needed to turn it into a bike that I could actually ride.

This, of course, meant yet more happy hours on the internet, comparing the price and weight of gears, saddles, tyres, handlebars and everything else. I became obsessive about how I could shave off a few grams here and there, but realised that there were several occasions when I nearly spent the price of a decent night out just so I'd have pedals that saved the equivalent weight of a Mars bar (or by spending a bit more, maybe even a pork pie).

After staring at my all but useless frame for a few months, and having exhausted every component combination that was within (or just outside) my budget, I was finally in a position to take it to be built into a bike. Although in years gone by I could easily have put a bike together, the technology had changed enough for me to want to pass the responsibility of assembly to a professional. A week later, I got a phone call to say it was ready and arranged to go and collect it.

I felt exactly as excited as I had as a child waiting for Christmas when I set out in the car to bring it home. We had some friends staying with us at the time, so I knew that even once I'd got the bike back to the house, I wasn't going to be able to take it out on the road for another few, tantalising days.

When I got back, I proudly wheeled my new bike up the path and took it inside. I had hoped that now my wife and the children could see it as a fully functioning machine, they'd be at least a little bit impressed, but they simply agreed with me that it was 'quite nice', and left it at that. I didn't really care – I was now the owner of a Colnago, and if my wife, children, friends and anyone else didn't want to get excited about that, it was their problem.

My long awaited first ride on my dream bike finally arrived. It was spring time so the winter salt had long been washed from the roads – I wasn't going to risk anything corrosive dulling the shiny paintwork and new components. I set off, nervously at first, but delighted that the bike did actually feel as good as I'd hoped. It felt light and responsive, and much more comfortable than the bike it was replacing. I had been a bit worried that it might not feel any different, and that I was setting myself up for a big disappointment, a bit like the first time I spent more than four pounds on a bottle of wine, and found I couldn't tell the difference between it and the usual plonk I generally drank at the time.

The only big disappointment came as I struggled up Norwood Edge, the hill near where I live that so often makes up part of my rides. At this point I had never ridden up it, and the fact that I was on my new bike meant I was looking forward to the challenge slightly more than I might otherwise have been. Or at least I wasn't actually dreading it, and got to its lower slopes in a state of blissful ignorance. I got about half way up and simply ground to a halt. As it was the first time I'd ever tried to ride up it, I probably shouldn't have been too disappointed, but as I slumped over my bike trying to get my breath, I couldn't help thinking that the first time shouldn't have been quite like this.

That incident aside, I was delighted with my new bike. I didn't dare risk keeping it in the shed so it lived by my desk in my study. This arrangement had the added advantage that if I got bored whilst I was supposed to be working, I could occupy myself with a bit of extra polishing on the few parts of it that weren't already shiny enough in which to see my reflection.

Now that I'd got myself a flashy new machine, I began to encounter one unforeseen problem. It was all very well to be overtaken by other cyclists when I had the appearance of an ungainly middle aged man on a cheap bike. If I met other cyclists whilst I was out, I noticed that they tended to take a sneaky glance at the bike I was riding. I must admit that I do the same. Seeing my cheap first bike, they didn't seem to have any need to comment on it, or to increase the speed at which they were riding alongside me. Now that I was on something that suggested I knew what I was doing, I was sometimes a bit embarrassed that I didn't have the ability to match, and frequently found myself having to make a lot more effort than I was used to. There seemed a certain irony in the fact that when I was a teenager, searching for every last little detail, a flashy bike, like the one I now owned, might have actually have been of some benefit to me, but now that I could afford that very bike, it was really just an extravagance.

I'm pretty sure that I'm not alone in this. A lot of those middle aged, middle class cyclists that are part of the 'new golf' brigade are much the same. I frequently see bikes that wouldn't look out of place on the start line of the Tour de France being ridden by people who wouldn't look out of place on the start line of a 'over sixties over weight grandparents' race at a school sports day. They have the same kit and power, speed, distance and power measuring devices as the best equipped professionals, all so that they can go home and look at what they've done on their home computer and then share all this information with the rest of the world via the internet. The appetite for new shiny bits of bike related paraphernalia amongst this group is insatiable, and all this equipment is far more than everyone needs. The latest must have device is the power meter. This allows even more in-depth analysis of each ride, with even more numbers to look at and ponder over, which can all be turned into colourful graphs to share with your friends. I haven't yet succumbed to buying one, but I'm sure they will continue to fall in price to the point where they are as common as a simple bike computer is now, and as I already have a GPS computer that tells me more than I need to know, it will only be a small step for me to buy yet more devices that let me amass enough statistics about my cycling to reinforce the fact that I'm really not very good at it.

I know that I have no real need for a GPS enabled bike computer that can measure how fast I'm going, how high I've climbed, tell me what my heart rate was at any given point in my ride, and how many calories I've burned whilst doing so (although the calories burned can help in my Pork Pie Allowance calculations). These little devices can probably provide more information than NASA used to send men to the moon. The most important statistics are, after all, the most basic ones. Number one and number two being; how many bikes you own, and how often you ride them.

I also don't need a carbon fibre Italian bike, or the latest and most fashionable wrap-around sunglasses. Just like everyone else who gets on a bike every Sunday to go out with their friends, owning totally unnecessary equipment is all part of the fun. Come to think of it, I might just get myself some new sunglasses next time I'm in a bike shop. A nice expensive pair that I can leave in a cafe somewhere, or drop out of my back pocket into the path of a passing car, safe in the knowledge that, for a while at least, my eyes were as well protected as the most cosseted pair of eyes in the professional peloton.

Stage 8
Learning How to Ride a Bike Properly

Having spent as much money as I could on equipment, and done everything within my will and ability to hone my body into that of an athlete, I had reached the stage where I was as well equipped, at least technically, as I possibly could be in terms of being a competent cyclist.

It had been many years ago, back in the days of Dicco and I sharing our dreams that I had realised that I was never going to make it as a professional cyclist. I could easily have blamed the fact that most of the best riders of my age had parents who were keen cyclists and had therefore practically been born on a bike, giving them an advantage that I never had. I could have blamed the fact that I never had access to the best equipment, even though my Carlton Professional was actually a pretty decent bike. I could have blamed the fact that I concentrated as much, if not more, on getting my homework done than I had on training (hardly true). The simple truth was, I simply wasn't good enough. I never had, and never would, have that natural *something else* that the true greats in any sport possess.

So what is this *something else*? I was once at a sales conference with work and one of the things that inevitably make up a large part of these types of event is some kind of team building activity. Often this involves an embarrassing aspect, such as wearing fancy dress in public in order to increase your self-confidence. Then there is usually an activity that makes you think as part of a team. Raft building seems to be a particular favourite, which, in my experience develops 'team spirit' through a process of arguing, cheating and being put at serious risk of death by drowning.

On this particular occasion we were all summoned to the hotel tennis court. As we nursed serious hangovers, of the type that can only be achieved by being given access to an endless supply of free foreign beer, we watched as one of our bosses demonstrated part of our task for the morning. This involved dribbling and kicking a football through a series of hoops and obstacles, before we'd be allowed, as a team, to progress to the next stage of the activities.

The man demonstrating this, Tom Easton, had played football professionally in Scotland. He'd played for the sort of teams that regularly feature in 'Final Score' each Saturday – Hamilton Academicals, Partick Thistle, Queen of the South - all names that seemed very familiar to me. He'd stopped playing because it was costing him more in bus fares to get to matches than he was being paid to play. Yet, as he walked around that tennis court he clearly possessed *something else* in his ability to kick a ball. Throughout his short demonstration, he looked around our group, keeping eye contact with various people, whilst explaining what he wanted us to do. At the same time, the ball he had at his feet barely seemed to touch the ground. He never lost control of it for even the briefest second, he passed it from foot to foot as easily as he breathed and spoke. It was simply second nature to him.

Tom probably has lots of reasons why he's not a famous ex-footballer, but on that day it was obvious that he had a certain something that only a fortunate few are really blessed with, a natural, almost genetic, ability to perform a task that many of us find difficult in such a way that he barely had to think about it.

Surely though, riding a bike is different to this? After all, you only have to stay upright and pedal as hard as you can, for as long as you can. It seems obvious that there isn't an aspect of cycling that can't easily be mastered by anyone. Surely, anyone can ride a bike?

This might be true for the simple task of learning to keep your balance while maintaining some degree of forward momentum, but there is a massive difference between those who have natural ability on a bike, and those who don't.

There have been lots of bits of research into the physiology of great athletes, including cyclists. The five times Tour de France winner Miguel Indurain had a lung capacity that defied belief, it was said to be twenty per cent bigger that a 'normal' man of his size. The advantage to this is pretty obvious – it allows the body to make better use of the oxygen that allows a high degree of effort. Of course, these days, this sort of thing gets measured scientifically, and is known as VO2 max.

Measuring VO2 max is something that happens for most top cyclists to help them prepare their correct training plan. If you're blessed with a high VO2 max, you're very lucky because it means you're already well on the way to success. You'll obviously still need to train, but training can only increase VO2 max by a few per cent. If you're VO2 max is very low, I'm afraid that you can train as hard as you like, but Mother Nature has decreed that life as an athlete will be much harder for you than for some other lucky individuals. When Lance Armstrong had only just started training again after his cancer, his VO2 max was found to be as high as that of a well-trained college athlete, so he was starting his road to recovery from a very high base, not that this in any way detracts from his achievements (the fact that he was a drug cheat does that), but it does at least make mere mortals like me feel that we've got at least some excuse for our inadequacies.

There have been countless occasions when I have come across elderly men out on their bikes. They usually seem to be riding old fashioned, hand built bikes, and keeping a pace which could best be described as 'stately'. But it's always obvious that these men have ridden so many miles over the years that their bikes almost seem part of them. Their pedalling action is so smooth and efficient that they barely seem to be making any effort. When they reach a hill, their expression and breathing doesn't seem to change. If its summer and they're in shorts, they expose legs that look like carved ebony, legs that have a million miles of roads in them. This fluid and efficient pedalling style can be developed, but some people just possess it naturally. The first time they ride a bike, they look like it is something that they've done all their lives.

Watching the professionals on television gives you a chance to see how smoothly and effortlessly they seem to pedal. When the road starts to go uphill, their level of effort doesn't seem to change in any way. By watching the way they position themselves on a bike it's easy to try and emulate this yourself. This can help a lot, and make riding long distances a bit easier, but it still doesn't always mean you're really riding like a pro. You might have the right position on your bike, you might have a replica team outfit and a replica team bike, but the chances are, even with a lot of training and practice, you'll *still* look like an amateur.

So what can you do to really complete your ensemble and make all the people that see you out on the road think that they've seen someone who really knows what they're doing?

It's important to plan ahead – looking like a pro starts before you actually get onto the saddle. Once you've got your cycling gear on, you don't just jump on your bike. There are countless pictures of top class cyclists relaxing before the start of a Tour stage or other big race. They usually sit reading a newspaper, sipping a drink. This is probably the only part of the pro-look that the average cyclist can get right. Although, to get this truly right, the only drink should be espresso, and the newspaper should either be the French *'L'Equipe'* or the Italian *'La Gazetta della Sport'*. Ideally you should be sitting at a table outside, in warm sunshine. So in the UK, sipping a mug of tea and reading *'The Daily Star'* in a transport cafe while you wait for the rain to stop, doesn't quite present the same image as sitting, tanned and relaxed, under an awning to shade yourself from the morning sun. And even the most ardent fashionista of cycling would have to admit that making a special effort to buy copies of newspapers you can't understand, just so you can look cool, is taking your obsession a bit too far.

If you are to sit in the sunshine reading a newspaper (even if it's not a foreign one), you'll need to wear sunglasses. Mirrored ones look best, and should be worn as long as it's not actually dark. The reason is obviously because you'll rarely see a pro without mirrored sunglasses on his face, but if anyone asks, you're not only wearing sunglasses to protect your eyes from harsh UV rays (which doesn't sound too convincing on a wet dull day), but also to keep road grit out of your eyes. Once you get off your bike it's important to remove your expensive mirrored sunglasses, but equally important never to put them down anywhere. Sunglasses that aren't being worn should be slotted into the air vents at the front of your helmet, and if you're not wearing your helmet (for example in a pub or cafe), they should be worn across your head, ideally over some kind of bandana. The bandana is there to absorb the sweat inside your helmet of course, and not just as something on which to display your sunglasses.

Leg shaving is something of a contentious issue amongst cyclists. I've yet to hear a truly convincing explanation as to why top cyclists do this. Some of the reasons given are that it's more aerodynamic, thus saving a microscopic bit of effort, others say that it's because you're likely to fall off your bike quite often and a wound on a shaven leg is easier to clean than on a hairy one. Logic would suggest that both these reasons justify shaved arms, which is something you never see on a cyclist. The other reason often given is that it makes massage easier, which is slightly more plausible. All these reasons may have some truth in the world of a professional seeking every possible marginal gain, but they hardly apply to the hobby cyclist like me. I have shaved my legs in the past. In mine and Dicco's early racing days we did it because the pros did it, and because everyone else in our club did it. When I shaved my legs a couple of years ago, it was almost as a dare. I must admit it felt better when I was on the bike, but I didn't feel to be going any faster, never had a massage, and was fortunate enough not to have a fall during the time my legs were smooth, so all the professional excuses didn't apply to me. However, it looked better, and in all honesty I think that's the reason so many cyclists shave their legs, and if, as a middle aged man puffing and wheezing your way to fitness every weekend, you decide to shave your legs, you'll look more like a pro. Just don't be too surprised if you have a wife that doesn't like it.

With all the modern health advice about the dangers of over

exposure to the sun, it's important to remember that as a cyclist who spends many hours out in the fresh air, you're at an increased risk of harm from the sun's rays. This obviously means that once you've made sure you've applied the right type of cream to your nether regions to protect from the dangers of saddle sores, you must turn your mind to the areas of skin that will be exposed to the sun. High factor sun cream is a must, but as well as giving protection, this also allows you to increase your 'pro-cyclist disguise' by developing the 'cyclists tan'. This can only be viewed to full effect by the swimming pool on your family holiday, when, just for once, you will be as badly dressed as everyone else. A true cyclist's tan means that you'll have white hands (although your fingertips will be tanned because of your fingerless cycling gloves), chestnut brown (or pink if you are fair skinned) arms, a milky white torso, and legs that are tanned from about half way down the thigh to just above the ankle, giving the illusion that you always wear white socks. (This effect may also be enhanced if you've shaved your legs, just like the pros do).

So, once you've got your sunglasses on at the right angle, your sun tan cream on your arms and legs (shaved or otherwise), you can finally get on your bike. Whilst professionals make use of experts to ensure that their saddles and handlebars are set to precisely the right height and angle, there are other aspects to your position on a bike which can help add to the illusion created by a mere mortal who wants to looks like a pro. When going uphill, tilting the head slightly to one side and grimacing, with a slight hint of the sort of sneer that Elvis Presley used to employ will give you a look more like that of the Tour de France contender who's photo you admired in many magazines. Lowering the zip on the front of your jersey, or even opening it fully, adds to the effect. One other thing to remember when going uphill, is that despite the fact that the best place to hold the handlebars is either on the flat top section, or the brake lever hood, you'll look a lot cooler by standing on the pedals and holding onto the dropped, lowest section of your bars, just like the great Italian climber Marco Pantani used to. (A big gold earring would complete the picture nicely). It's also important to remember *where* to look. In most cases, when I'm going uphill, I look at the square metre of road directly ahead of my front wheel. This is generally because I'm almost physically unable to look anywhere else, and I have to try to remember to look up from time to make sure I don't run into anything. If I was doing my ultimate 'pro-look', I'd have my eyes firmly on a point in the far distance, thus giving the illusion that the summit of a famous mountain is just coming into sight.

All this is especially important if, whilst riding in any type of event, you see someone on the side of the road who wants to take your photograph. These pictures can usually be bought afterwards, so you want to get the best value for your money. The most important thing of all to remember if you do see a photographer is to *never* look at the camera – after all, how many pictures of riders have you seen when they've given the photographer a nice smile? You need to look like you're suffering, and to have been in too much pain to even notice someone taking your picture.

Athletes from many types of sport often look toned and healthy in the sort of tabloid photos that expose their illicit holiday romances from time to time. Many even get used in photographs to promote anything from health drinks to after shave, showing impressive sets of abdominal muscles under their toned and waxed skin. Not so professional cyclists. They tend to look malnourished and skinny. Even the sprint specialists on the Tour de France, who are usually among the heavier riders, carry barely any body fat.

I've always been pretty thin, but a serious summer of training for the Etape one year helped me get down to about sixty five kilos, or just over ten and a half stone, which was the lightest I'd been for years. I was pretty pleased about this, and even managed to convince myself that it was making me climb hills faster, and noticed that I could see a few extra bones when I looked in the mirror. I'd probably managed to get even thinner during the course of the big day – nearly two hundred kilometres, finishing at the top of Col du Tourmalet. A group of us were using a borrowed van to transport the bikes about during our trip. As there were five people, and only three seats in the front of the van, my pal Al and I had volunteered to ride in the back whilst we drove into Pau one day for something to eat. It was hot and sunny and the van had no air conditioning, so we felt as if we were being slowly roasted. Because I was so hot and tired, I took my t-shirt off and rolled it up to use as a makeshift pillow whilst I had a nap. Whilst I slept Al took a photo of me. When I saw it later, it looked like the sort of picture that humanitarian charities use to launch an appeal. I could easily have passed as a victim of man's inhumanity to man, and looked an extra from a film about a Japanese prisoner of war camp. But I also looked like I *almost* had the physique of a professional cyclist, even though, for my height, I would still have been considered heavy if I had lined up alongside a group of bare chested Tour de France riders. What it showed me was that, however thin I got, I was still too fat to look like a pro.

Having honed your body to the emaciated and hungry look of a professional, you do of course need to make sure that you're dressed properly. As far as clothing yourself like a pro is concerned, I think I'm of the opinion that you should only wear a professional team jersey if you're paid to do so, and you should only wear a yellow jersey if you're actually the leader of the Tour de France. If you want to feel like part of a group, join a club and wear your club jersey with pride. At least it's unlikely that the design of your club jersey will change very often, thus ensuring a few extra years of use. It is even less likely that one of your club mates will fall foul of the cycling authorities, thus leaving you in the position of wearing a jersey that shows you support a drug cheat. The only possible exception to this is if you opt for a truly retro jersey, of a design that's at least thirty years old. This is a good way of showing that you've known about cycling for a long time, and that you are the sort of person who can easily bore people in the pub by talking about obscure events, ones that took place when 'men were men', and it always rained, and riders had to repair their own bikes with their bare hands, and ride through the snow to win a race, then ride home on their bikes, rather than in a team bus. The ultimate retro jerseys are of obscure Flemish teams that no one has ever heard of, ideally from a club in a town with an unpronounceable name, displaying the logo of a local car dealership or bike shop.

As an amateur you'll always have the option of going home if the weather really is bad, but there will be times when, with your bike polished, your freshly laundered kit on, and your last pre-ride espresso drunk, you'll actually throw your leg over your bike and set off for a ride. With a bit of luck, you'll be able to meet up with a few friends and really make the most of cycling as a pastime. Riding in a group is a much more enjoyable way of cycling, and presents the opportunity to make new friends, have a more sociable time on your bike, and of course cause an argument by doing something wrong.

There are a few simple rules to the art of group cycling, many of which can be copied from the riders you see on television. After all, the Tour de France peloton is, on some days, like a big club ride until the last few kilometres. The most important thing for an amateur to remember is to keep an even pace, preferably riding two abreast and keeping your handlebars level with those of the rider next to you. Gradually increasing the pace and moving ahead is known as 'half wheeling' and is seen as a cardinal sin amongst regular riders. When you've had enough of riding at the front, move out of the way, drop back and let someone else take up the pace. Don't think for a minute that you're being helpful by sprinting to the front of the group to do your turn in the wind. All that will happen is that you'll be going too fast and everyone in the group will have to go faster and work harder, which is the opposite to the effect you're really trying to achieve. It's also important to keep as close as you can to the rider in front.

One of the biggest benefits of being in a group is that you can make use of the rider in front's slipstream. This means you're expending much less effort, but still keeping the same pace, and if you let a gap open up in the line, you and everyone behind you will have to work harder. Other than that, all you need to remember is not to change direction too suddenly, not to clear your nostrils without making sure you're not going to spray anyone, make sure you warn people about traffic approaching, point out any obstructions such as potholes and parked cars, and tell the group if anyone gets left behind. It's really all very simple.

It's up to you whether or not you think any of the above is true, or if you want to alter your riding in a way as a result of learning from the experiences of a middle aged man returning to the world of club cycling. At best, it will make you look a little less amateurish, and a little more like you know what you're doing. At worst, you will be able to hold a slightly qualified opinion about other people you see out on the road after you have done something that upsets them.

This difference between 'us and them', between the true thoroughbreds and the mere workhorses, was brought home to me the year that the Tour de France came to Yorkshire. In the months before the race the occasional professional could be seen out on the roads I ride on regularly. Even from a distance, these men stood out. They just looked different. Even if the best of local riders had donned the very same kit, and ridden the very same bike down the very same stretch of road, alongside the professional rider, it would have been obvious who was who. The true professionals just have something that sets them apart.

So even though I have come to realise that I should always have known that I was never going to be counted amongst the great names of cycling, I have a least learned a few useful bits and pieces over the years, so that, to all but the most discerning observer, I almost know how to ride a bike properly.

Stage 9
Dreams Come True

Like Christmas, or your annual summer holiday, things have a habit of coming around much quicker than you think they might. It had been early December when I had booked myself, Paul and Carol a place each in the Etape du Tour. In March Paul had started training, and as the weather warmed up we had found ourselves doing more and more miles, and suddenly able to hold a conversation whilst riding up hills that had left us out of breath only a few weeks earlier.

I had done my first ride of over one hundred miles in May – the Etape du Dales sportive in the Yorkshire Dales, a brutally hard event made even harder by strong winds and rain. I had only entered to make sure I could manage the distance, and was pleased to have got all the way around. May passed into June, then all of a sudden, it was time to finalise our arrangements and buy the last of our supplies of energy gels and spare inner tubes and do our packing.

One of the biggest headaches about travelling abroad to ride in an event is putting your shiny new bike onto a plane, and worrying about how badly damaged it will be when it comes along the luggage carousel at the other end of your flight. I had heard lots of horror stories about people unpacking their bikes to find buckled wheels, damaged gears and cracked frames, so had decided to buy a hard flight case. It seemed huge when it was delivered, but it actually took quite a bit of practice to get my bike, wheels removed, into it, without having to force the lid closed by getting one of my children to sit on it. I was reasonably happy with the old t-shirts, tea towels and bits of pipe lagging that I had used to protect my bike, and could even still lift the box without too much difficulty. A local bike shop had given Paul one of the cardboard boxes that they have bikes delivered in, and we spent an entertaining couple of hours taking his bike to bits and working out how to get it packed. At last, we were ready.

Setting off to ride the Tour de France (or at least one stage of it) turned out to be a very different scenario to the one I had imagined with Dicco. Instead of kissing my podium girl wife goodbye on the steps of our house somewhere in the South of France, to be collected by a team car and whisked away to the start town, my middle aged pal and I drove up to Leeds Bradford airport on a drizzly morning to catch a flight to Nice, laden down with heavy bike boxes and a small suit case each of kit.

We met Carol at the airport. She seemed to have had a bit less success with her bike packing efforts than Paul and I, because she was carrying a front wheel in her hand. She didn't seem as neurotically worried as we were when it disappeared beyond the baggage check on its way to the plane.

My Mum and Dad were already on holiday near Nice, and met us off the plane so we could borrow their car for the drive over to Pau. My dad doesn't believe in parting with money unless absolutely necessary, so we found him waiting in the 'Kiss and Fly' section of the car park, which meant that we only had a couple of minutes to load our stuff into the car before we would incur parking charges. Dad just had time to demonstrate the complexity of electric windows to Paul, before we waved goodbye and made our way to the auto-route in the direction of Pau.

It was a beautiful sunny afternoon and we passed the time eating sandwiches that my mum had left for us in the car, and talking about what lay ahead. We were still full of bravado and excitement, it was only as the mountains (which looked like clouds against the horizon) came into view, that we started to feel a bit nervous. As we neared Pau, we spotted more and more cars with bikes on roofs or stuffed into the rear seats in place of families who would probably have quite liked to spend a couple of days in the Pyrenees in July.

Our accommodation was in what looked like a university halls of residence. It was clean but basic, at least the room was big enough for all our kit to be spread liberally around without us running the risk of serious injury whilst making a nocturnal trip to the loo. We decided to leave the job of reassembling our bikes until morning, because the thought of the consequences of any fatigue induced mistakes could be so great. Also what we really wanted was to go out for steak and chips and a few beers.

Pau is a beautiful town, so after a few phone calls for directions, and a few more for re-directions, we found our friends in a restaurant which gave a fantastic view toward the mountains. Paul stood on the veranda of the restaurant, and fixed his eyes on the distant peaks then he turned and looked at our assembled group, composed largely of men in their forties and fifties. 'Fuck me' was all he could say.

We ordered cold beers, filled ourselves up on bread, steak and chips, washed that down with a glass or three of rough red wine, had a couple of extra beers and made our way back to our 'hotel'. Paul was keen to carry on the night's festivities, but being a highly self-disciplined athlete, I decided that half a bottle of red wine and five pints of gassy French lager was probably enough.

We were up fairly early the next day, and having managed to get our bikes back together without too much trouble, assembled in the car park for a warm up ride, following a guide from the tour company who had organised our trip.

It's hard to describe how I felt. Ever since I was a boy I had dreamed of cycling in France, on the same roads as I had read about week after week in the cycling magazines that consumed most of my pocket money. Finally, here I was, clipping into my pedals to set off doing just that. Even though this was just a short warm up ride, I couldn't stop smiling. It was obvious from the reactions of anyone we passed that they knew why we were there. We got lots of shouts of 'Chapeau' from people by the road side, and waves of encouragement from almost all the other riders we saw.

In the afternoon we had to go and sign on for the event itself. We took a coach to the local outdoor cycle track where there was a huge village of tents and marquees. We joined a long but fast moving line of nervous cyclists, collected our free rucksack, containing a free t-shirt, free water bottle, free energy gel and about half a ton of useless tourist information. We had a quick sort through this, and dumped, in the nearest bin, all the bits we didn't want.

After signing for our numbers, we spent the next couple of hours looking at the sort of stalls that wouldn't look out of place at an English agricultural show. We could have bought local jams, local meat, local cheese, local cider. Local just about anything. Instead I bought myself a commemorative cycling top, and far more extra energy gels than I would ever need.

In the evening we had our first chance to meet with the rest of the people in our tour group. We were taken to a local restaurant for a meal. This was typically French – especially as there was a bottle of wine on each table. Sat next to us was a group of triathletes from a club in London. One of the men, who seemed to see himself as something of a group leader, announced to the table that none of them would be drinking any alcohol before the event, so they wouldn't be needing the wine. As the bottles were already open, and realising that our hosts may be offended if it was left untouched, Paul and I offered to sort out the 'problem' for them by disposing of the wine in a way that wouldn't upset anyone. I'm sure the extra calories did us good.

I could have understood this pious attitude if these people were seriously challenging to win some major event, but considering we were supposed to be there to have fun, and enjoy the whole experience, this self-denial seemed pointless. (I later passed one of them on the road, and he looked like he needed a glass of wine to help perk him up a bit).

We still had another day to wait before the event itself. This should have been time when we relaxed and rested, but nervousness and anxiety meant that we made endless unnecessary adjustments to our bikes, went for a walk that we didn't really want to go on and generally wasted energy that we should have been saving. We went out to a cafe for lunch, and all ordered omelette and chips. The waiter offered us wine, but when we followed the example of the triathletes from London and ordered coke instead, he gave a huge Gallic shrug and almost spat 'Pah – les Sportifs!' before turning away in disgust to get our drinks.

Once we got back, Paul and I must have tidied and rearranged our stuff about a dozen times before it was finally time to get onto a mini bus to be taken for our evening meal. This was predictably a huge bowl of pasta, accompanied by as much bread as we could physically eat. It wasn't a bad meal – but no one seemed to enjoy it. The reason was that, sitting on a terrace in France naturally means that you want plenty of wine to wash down your food and have plenty of time to relax and enjoy yourself. Instead, we restrained ourselves to one small glass of wine each, just to aid our digestion and the noisy conversation you would usually expect was absent – everyone was a bit subdued, thinking of the day ahead, and of the 4am.start.

As a child on family holidays in France, one of the things I always looked forward to was breakfast – no Corn Flakes and toast like at home, but piles of croissants and pain au chocolat, washed down with orange juice or milky hot chocolate, usually sitting outside in the sunshine. On the morning of the Etape though, we were shivering in the darkness at 4am trying to force feed ourselves as much as we possibly could. We barely spoke; we all just looked down at the food we were trying to consume and forced ourselves to eat and eat and eat. Eventually the call came for us to go outside to the coach and, still under cover of darkness, we set of for the start.

I tried to have a nap during the journey, but my attempts at sleep were fruitless. I consoled myself by eating another banana and watching as the sun rose above the horizon. This looked beautiful, until I realised that in a couple of hours' time, I'd be trying to ride my bike over the mountains that were slowly emerging in the light of the dawn.

By the time we'd retrieved our bikes and got to our place at the start, the sun was up and the air was starting to warm. All the riders were divided into groups according to their number, which meant Paul and I had to say goodbye to Carol and then go off and join the thousands of other riders filling the roads behind the start line.

With still about half an hour to start time, our nervous state meant that we spent most of our time holding each other's bikes so that one of us could climb over the fence at the side of the road to go water the bushes a bit more. Thousands of other people in the same state of anxiety as us meant that the town council of Maurenx could probably leave the sprinklers switched off for the day. There were portaloos provided as well, but these had the sort of smell that reminded me of the toilets at a rock festival, so I was glad I'd been able to deal with that particular need before I'd got on the coach to the start. (Up until the previous evening, bowel movements had taken up nearly as much conversational time as how many gels we thought we'd need).

Despite all the nervousness, there was a carnival atmosphere among the riders. Terrible French pop music was playing over a public address system and there was an ongoing commentary from various local dignitaries, some of which even I could understand, with my only slightly better than schoolboy French. (I usually find that my ability to speak French increases directly in proportion to how much alcohol I've drunk – and as I'd only drunk coffee and orange juice so far that day, I wasn't at my best from a linguistic perspective).

I certainly understood the countdown to the seven o'clock start – '*cinq, quatre, trois, deux, un... Allez!!!!*' A big cheer from many of the riders, then... nothing! We were so far back from the start line that we had to wait about twenty minutes before a wave of clicking sounds, as riders engaged their shoes into their pedals, finally meant that we could get moving.

It took a couple of minutes to negotiate the winding route to the proper start line. There was a reasonable crowd shouting encouragement and politely applauding from the road side. Finally, we passed under a gantry, there was a 'bleep' as we rode over the electronic timing mat, there was a sudden increase in speed, and I was at last fulfilling my biggest boyhood dream. I was riding the Tour de France! Me! Riding the Tour! At least that's how it felt. I freely admit that reality was slightly different, and that in all honesty I was actually riding an amateur cycling event in France. But that didn't matter to me. I looked up at the sky, looked around at the other riders and at the spectators on the road side, just for one moment, everything I had dreamed about as a second-rate schoolboy racer had come true.

I looked around for Paul, but there were so many riders around that I couldn't see him. I didn't want my dream to end in the first kilometre, so decided instead to concentrate on those around me and see if I could settle into a group and get going at a reasonable pace. A few minutes later I heard a 'Hi mate' from over my left shoulder, and there was Paul, albeit briefly, alongside me. He was only there for a few seconds, and soon disappeared into the crowd of riders, and I didn't see him again until the end of the day.

The first few kilometres took us through the outskirts of Maurenx, and up a short hill, which, somewhat surprisingly, was steep enough for some riders to be pushing their bikes. I couldn't help thinking that if this small rise in the road meant that they were already walking, the big climbs later in the route were going to mean that they would really be struggling. A few minutes later I saw a rider at the side of the road looking in disbelief at the remains of his front wheel, which looked to be almost bent in two.

There were people going at all different speeds, some taking it slowly and others weaving at high speed in and out of groups of riders to try to get themselves as far forward in the pack as they could. It took me a while to remember that because it is natural to ride on the right hand side of the road abroad, the faster ones would naturally want to pass on my left shoulder, unlike at home. After a few minutes we were out of town, gradually the sheer volume of competitors started to thin out and there seemed to be more room on the road and I felt able to relax a bit.

This was supposed to be a mountain stage of the tour, and it wasn't long before we reached the foot of the first climb, the Col d'Ichere. This wasn't a climb I had heard of, but it was still my first experience of a real Tour de France mountain. As the road started to go uphill, I still had a feeling of disbelief that I was actually riding a real 'Col'. The road was narrow and gritty, but the gradient didn't feel too bad. I could see the road curling its way up the mountain ahead and at each turn it looked to be getting steeper and steeper, but as I climbed higher, it never seemed to get as steep as it looked. The landscape was made up of meadow and small grassy fields, but as we neared the top it gradually became more barren, similar to the moors over which Paul and I had ridden for so many miles during our training. At last, we rounded a corner and there were people and cars by the side of the road. There were a few flags and banners set into the ground, and I realised that we'd reached the top. I coasted along for a few seconds, and then with what seemed like only a few turns of the pedals, I was on my way down the other side of the mountain.

The road was similar to the one we had climbed – narrow, winding and with an uneven, gravel strewn surface. It was the sort of hill that I would have gone down carefully if I'd been on my own, never mind surrounded by so many other cyclists, all of whom seemed either very nervous or suicidally over confident. Behind me I heard the unmistakable sound of someone crashing – cracking, crushing and scraping as bike and rider part company, along with cries of warning from anyone near enough to have seen what had happened. I didn't dare look around, but instead kept my eyes on the road ahead and my fingers covering my brake levers.

I'd spoken to Dicco on the phone just before we'd set out on our trip, and he'd warned me about the next climb, which was one I had read about many times – the Col de Marie Blanque. He'd described it as 'a bastard of a climb', but I reassured myself by remembering the belief we'd both held as school boys – that he was a sprinter and I was a climber, so I thought I'd probably be OK.

The road up the Marie Blanque ascends through a lot of trees, and in July this means the heat seems all the more oppressive.

There were so many riders that the pace of the masses of people trying to get up the climb became gradually slower and slower, until we all found ourselves at a standstill. It was bitterly disappointing to have to dismount and walk, but at least I reassured myself with the fact that it wasn't because I *wanted* to get off, but that I had no choice because the road was blocked. The heat meant that there were plumes of steam rising from the sweaty riders clip-clopping their way up the road. Finally, as we neared the top, the road widened and everyone could get back on their bikes, and proudly ride over the crest of the mountain, ready for another spectacular descent. This time, the road surface was good, and I was able to see bend after bend snaking out down toward the bottom of the valley. This meant I could enjoy the experience a bit more and I gradually started to feel more confident. Every time I started to think to myself that I was doing quite well at going downhill quickly, someone would fly past me at the sort of speed that suggested I was standing still. It was terrifying to see just how fast some of these people were going. Even passing several bits of shattered bike on one bend did little to dampen their spirits. I was surprised that such long sections of downhill were so tiring. My shoulders and the back of my neck began to ache, and I found myself having to sit up to ease the pain.

There were feeding areas on the route but I'd skipped the first one, by the time I arrived at the second, I knew I needed some more supplies. I was already sick of the taste of energy gels and my bottles were empty. The feed station was in a big car park and what struck me most was the sound of the place. There were thousands and thousands of discarded plastic mineral water bottles all over the ground, and everyone had to walk across them to get to the tables of food and drink. The sound of these plastic bottles being crushed underfoot was almost deafening.

Because of all the sweet flavoured energy gels I had eaten, I really wanted something with a savoury taste to eat, but the tables of the feeding station where spread with yet more gels, cakes, bananas and bottles of mineral water. I took a couple of bananas and four bottles of water and made my way back to where I had been forced to abandon my bike. I ate as much as I could, drank some water and used what was left to refill my own water bottles.

I looked around at everyone, had a bit of a stretch and kind of felt myself all over, almost as if I wanted to reassure myself that my whole body was still in working order. I realised that I actually didn't feel too bad. My shoulders ached a bit, but my legs felt OK, and getting back onto my bike wasn't too painful or uncomfortable.

I was about half way round. I found myself starting to feel quietly confident that I was going to be OK.

The sun was high and it was a beautiful summer's day. The road was gently downhill, I was feeling fit. It felt easy. I passed a sign saying that we'd already reached the hundred kilometre point. Feeling this good after this far meant the rest of the ride just wasn't going to be a problem. I thought to myself how the training had paid off. How all those rain soaked miles had been worth it. I was in a dream, and in that dream, I was a Tour de France rider, I was beginning to fool myself into thinking I knew what it meant to be a giant of the road.

Stage 10
Reality Bites

Whenever you watch someone perform a task for which they have an almost unnatural inbuilt ability, they always make it look easy. I've watched footballers (like my old colleague Tom Easton) who can keep a ball in the air for as long as they please (my personal 'keepie uppy' record is about four touches), and well remember the difficulty that contestants on television shows like those on 'The Generation Game' used to have doing something as apparently simple as using a potter's wheel to make a jug out of a ball of clay.

In many ways, it's just the same watching the way the professional cyclists maintain such high speeds without showing any signs of effort. I was having that feeling now, as the road was gently rolling, the sun was out, and I was feeling quietly proud of myself for having got this far, whilst still feeling relatively relaxed. I was happily convincing myself that the reason it didn't look hard on television was because it really wasn't that hard. I knew that the biggest mountain of the day still lay ahead, but as I'd found the first two climbs easier than I expected, I wasn't too concerned.

I'd read up on the Col d'Aubisque before setting off. Most people seemed to say that the climb is easy at first until you reach the town of Eaux-Bonnes, then becomes much more difficult for the next few kilometres before easing off towards the end. The one bit that really stuck in my mind was one rider's warning that the road passes a hotel at one point, and it looks as if you are at the top of the hill. By this time, he said, you will be on your last legs and will be mentally shattered as you pass the hotel only to find the road continues upwards toward the sky for another two kilometres. Armed with this knowledge, I still felt quietly confident.

I was still in this naive dream-like state as I finally got to the bottom of the mountain. A climb I had watched many times on television and one of the most fabled in the history of the Tour de France. There were markers along the side of the road counting down each kilometre. The climb is eighteen kilometres long and it didn't seem to take me long to reach the 'Sommet 15 kilometre' sign. This still seemed easy. The local council had obviously taken advantage of the impending arrival of the Tour itself by blowing all their resources on tarmac, so the surface was perfectly smooth. I got talking to an English rider who asked how I was feeling. I told him I felt fine, but somewhere at the back of my mind, I was starting to worry. I was worrying that I was feeling so good and that the old saying 'pride comes before a fall' was about to come true in some dramatic fashion.

I looked at the hill which was rearing up above my left shoulder. I had to crane my neck as far as I could, until I could just about see the town high above. It looked like it had been balanced on a precipice, as if it could tumble into the valley at any time. It looked high, higher than I could really comprehend. The English chap was still alongside me and seemed keen on talking. He wanted to talk about his pace, his gearing, how fast he was going to climb and various other technical things that usually get boring after about five minutes in the pub, never mind when you're trying to ride up a mountain. I wondered if he was one of those annoying people who don't realise that there's more to life than talking incessantly about such things and being generally irritating, and considered pushing him off his bike to shut him up, a thought that was perhaps a little harsh at this stage.

The 'easy' part of the climb ended as we rode into Eaux-Bonnes, which looked to be a lovely town, with a large square that would have probably been just the sort of place that most English people have in their minds when they think of a trip to France, the sort of place where you can while away an hour or too sipping nice coffee and watching the world go by. There was no time for me to do anything so relaxing, as a young female Gendarme waved us to the left, where the road rose steeply towards the next bit of the climb. My new found friend briefly stopped talking about chain rings and brake cables to ask her for a kiss, but she just gave him one of those 'in your dreams' type looks and continued to wave everyone in the direction we had just taken. I reconsidered my reluctance to push him off his bike, but decided instead just to try and ride away from him.

Spurred on by a desire for a bit of peace and quiet, I put in a bit of an extra effort and managed to shake him off, leaving him questioning anyone who would listen what their heart rate was or what gear they were in. I realised that I was starting to feel tired, and gradually began to comprehend why the mountain stages have such a tough reputation. I felt the energy disappear from my legs, my breathing became more laboured, and I realised that I had become strangely fascinated by watching the sweat bounce off my knees with each pedal stroke.

I wondered about stopping. Would it make me feel better? Would a couple of minutes rest allow me to recover and improve my pace enough to make up for the time it took to get my breath back? I really didn't want to stop – I was trying to preserve my pride more than anything but then remembered that I'd had to stop on the climb of the Marie Blanque, so stopping now wouldn't really make any difference as far as my pride was concerned. I was turning this idea over in my head as I rounded a corner and saw a line of other riders taking a break and resting in the shade. It was too much to resist. I convinced myself that just stopping once wouldn't be so bad, and coasted over to the side of the road.

I took a long swig of water and watched the other riders struggling past. A few more stopped for a rest, but instead of this making me feel less guilty about stopping, I started to feel sheepish and vaguely embarrassed. There was no option but to remount and set off again.

The trouble with stopping once is that it makes the idea of

stopping again so much more appealing. I had to fight the urge for another quick stop, just as when you try to fight the urge for another chocolate when you know you've had plenty, but there, looking at you, is that really nice one that you really like, and you think 'just one more can't do any harm' before resistance fails and you succumb to temptation. I stopped once more, just briefly and then started to feel well enough to think about the rest of the climb.

It didn't seem to take long to reach the hotel I'd read about. I noticed everyone around me put in an extra bit of effort as they reached what they thought was the top of the mountain. There was nothing I could do or say to stop them doing this, so I didn't feel guilty about laughing to myself as I saw the look of horror on their faces as the last bit of the mountain revealed itself. Another two kilometres that snaked its way upwards at what looked like a terrible gradient. In reality, it wasn't too bad, and before long I was flying down the other side, knowing that I'd got over the worst part of the day.

The last named climb was called the Col du Soulor. I'd never heard of it before, and it didn't look at all hard on the route profile I had in my pocket. I struggled a bit as I wound my way up, but as I rounded the last corner I was greeted with a sight that both took my breath away and made me smile in equal measure.

There was a crowd. Not just a tiny group of spectators looking out for loved ones to encourage them over the last peak of the day, but a huge tunnel of screaming and shouting fans, just like I'd seen on television. They formed what looked like two walls for me to ride through. As well as all the screaming and shouting, they were banging cowbells, and some were even running alongside me. It was as close to a real life Tour de France experience as I could have dreamed of. I tried my best to look nonchalant but couldn't stop myself grinning crazily. There was another rider just ahead of me, and the noise of the crowd gave me enough energy to overtake him, my shoulders clashing with people running by my side.

As quickly as the deafening noise had started, it was replaced by silence. I'm sure there can have been no more than a couple of hundred people, but it had felt like there were thousands. It was a moment that I really will never forget, it remains one of the most memorable things that has ever happened to me on a bike. I felt on top of the world. No more mountains today, just a descent and a couple of lumps between me and the finish.

I can't pretend that the two descents I'd done so far had been completed with any style or panache or that I'd managed to gain any time on anyone else whilst going down from the top of the Col d'Ichere or the Col de Marie Blanque, but I did feel a bit more confident on what was the last big downhill section of the day.

The course wound along an undulating valley road for the next few miles and, full of confidence, I managed to be keeping up a good pace. I felt the presence of another rider close behind me. This meant that I'd have someone to share the work with and after a few minutes I moved to one side, to let him come through and do his share of taking the full force of the wind. Nothing happened. He didn't appear. This is definitely bad form and very much not the done thing. I was a bit cross and looked over my shoulder, intending to make it clear to him that if he was going to slipstream me, he should at least do his turn on the front to give me a rest. I was amazed to see not just one rider who should have been doing his fair share of work, but a group of about ninety. None of them would come through, and as I moved further and further to the left, they all just followed suit. I did another few hundred metres on the front of the group, and then swung off once more. This time I slowed so much that the group began to glide past me, until I pushed my way into a space about twenty or so riders from the front.

I knew that we were getting into the final stages of the ride now. I swallowed yet more gel and took another look at the route card, which was by now only just legible through a gooey mess of gel and cake. Two small hills looked to be all that was left. The road had already risen at least once so I thought that nearly all the climbing must be over.

Buoyed on by confidence and relief, I kept up a brisk pace.

Blissful in my ignorance, I forgot that the Tour de France can be merciless and that the spirit of Henri Desgrange and his philosophy of making riders suffer is ever present.

We were waved up a turning to the left by a Gendarme, to my horror I saw that the road rose steeply ahead of me. The hill looked at least as hard as my local 'hard climb', Norwood Edge. I couldn't believe it. I realised that what looked like two small hills on the route card were in fact, going to be pretty hard. They only looked small because they were smaller than the mountains that had come before. Their size was purely relative.

Riders all around me looked dismayed by what was ahead. Suddenly out of the silence a strong Birmingham accent said 'Bloody hell, that's bloody outrageous that is'. It made me laugh out loud, but didn't make the hill any smaller.

The heat was oppressive by now, and I struggled on, swearing and cursing under my breath. The second of the two 'small' hills came soon after and was even harder. At one point a woman at the side of the road said *'six cent metre, six cent metres'*. The problem was I thought she said *'soixante metres'*. I realised the difference between sixty and six hundred metres pretty soon afterwards, but didn't realise my mistake quickly enough to stop me cursing the woman for being so cruel.

It was a wonderful feeling to crest that last hill, and the realisation dawned on me that I was going to fulfil my childhood dream, and finish a stage of the Tour de France. I found myself wanting to savour the moment, and wishing that the end of the day wasn't so close

I rode into the outskirts of Pau, full of excitement. The residents had obviously had enough of watching Lycra clad middle-aged men struggling past, and were trying to get on with their own tasks for the day. I remember feeling quite hurt that one woman I passed didn't even turn around to watch me ride by, just as I passed under the one kilometre to go banner. Soon I could hear the sound of the loudspeakers at the finish, and then there was just one tiny steep bit of road before we emerged into a square, and I coasted over the line. I had done it. I had finally ridden a stage of the Tour de France and I really didn't care if the residents of Pau didn't appreciate what I'd done. Not quite a giant of the road but I wasn't thinking of that now. I would be able to go home and watch the same stage on television and say, 'I've done that'.

Carol was sitting in the stands by the finish, she came over and gave me a very welcome hug. I found a couple of other friends who'd finished ahead of me and bought a beer from one of the stalls. I'm used to foreign beer tasting weak and soulless in comparison to the real ale I like at home, but this tasted even worse than I expected. After such a long day, I thought any beer would be like nectar but this was warm, weak and a bitter disappointment. I didn't really mind and sat soaking up the carnival like atmosphere as I waited for Paul to arrive. I gazed idly at my empty beer can, only to see that it was alcohol free. Probably sensible but I actually felt I deserved a proper drink right at that moment.

As Paul arrived he was swearing profusely having suffered four punctures along the way. He was delighted to have finished and we had a couple more beers before riding back to our hotel to freshen up and prepare to spend the evening celebrating our achievements.

After regrouping and showering everyone was looking forward to a night out to celebrate and re-live the day. We ate at a restaurant in a pleasant square and sat by a fountain. Everyone had their own stories to tell and we soon entered that typical post-ride euphoric mood. Long hard rides are much more enjoyable when you talk about them afterwards; all the talk of pain and suffering was soon replaced by wondering who'd be back next year, and what we'd do differently to make the day even better.

A hundred miles of cycling through the mountains tempered our desire for a really big night and we wandered, exhausted and happy, back to our hotel and slept what my mum would have called 'the sleep of the righteous'.

Back in England I ordered my souvenir photos, and wore my official 'Etape' jersey on short and enjoyable rides, outings that were done just to experience the simple pleasure of being on my bike. I wasn't worried about not riding far and it gave me a chance to show off my tan.

I'd only ever intended to do the Etape once as a way of fulfilling a dream. Somehow though, it still felt like something was unfinished, as if I'd only partially done what I had set out to do. I tried to rationalise these feelings in my mind, and to convince myself that there was no need to come back, no need to prove anything any longer.

When I thought about doing the Etape again, it made me think about all the training and expense it would entail. I needed an excuse NOT to come back, and finally thought of the perfect one. I'd only come back next year if there was to be a chance to ride on a really famous bit of road, the sort of road that sends a shiver down the spine of every cycling fan. Only a summit finish on Alpe d'Huez or Mont Ventoux would be enough to tempt me back.

The following October, on the day I knew the route of the next Etape would be announced, I was at a meeting when my phone bleeped to tell me I had a text. It was from Simon Old, one of the people who'd been in our group in Pau.

It simply said 'Alpe d'Huez'

Stage 11
No Cycling

I've always been something of a 'morning person'. Getting up early has never bothered me, or been something that I've found difficult. For someone with a hobby like cycling, its useful to be able to jump out of bed at the first sounding of the alarm and go out without disturbing the rest of your family as they take advantage of the weekend by having a bit of a lie in, the same way most normal people do.

One of my favourite early morning rides is when I'm on holiday. We usually stay in my parent's mobile home in France and my dad has a bike that he keeps there in a shed. I like to get up quietly, change into my kit and go out in the morning sunshine, before the heat of the day really takes hold and makes cycling too uncomfortable.

Almost as soon as I leave the gate, the road rises sharply. It climbs its way up the mountainside, passing holiday villas and through charming little villages. The topography means that there are plenty of opportunities for me to look over my shoulder and see how far I've come. It's surprising, and satisfying, to see how quickly I have gained height.

After forty minutes or so the village of Gourdon comes into view, perched precariously on a rocky outcrop. Pulling to the side of the road means I can fully take in the spectacular view all the way down to the sea, sometimes the early morning mist is slowly clearing from the parts of the valley where it has lingered, exposing lush looking pine woods, dotted with turquoise swimming pools.

There is a small café, where I can sit and enjoy a quick coffee before taking the same road back down the mountain, which takes about one third of the time it takes to climb, and get back before anyone else has stirred. I might even call for bread at the local bakery so I can sit on the veranda and wait for everyone else to get up so we can enjoy our breakfast in the sunshine. It is every bit as idyllic as it sounds.

Rising early at home in England usually means sneaking off for the club run or to drive to an event, usually having made sure all my stuff is ready and downstairs to minimise the disturbance caused by my shuffling about.

On one of those early mornings, I sneaked out of bed as quietly as I could and went downstairs to get ready to go out. As I tried to put on my jersey, I realised I couldn't raise my right arm without an agonizing pain shooting all around my back and shoulders. I couldn't even grip anything with my right hand. I was puzzled and worried in equal measure. I had never suffered anything like this before, apart from a bit of discomfort in my right hand when I had been twiddling away on my turbo trainer earlier in the week, which I had put down to my position being wrong.

Instead of spending my morning out cycling with friends, I spent a large part of it waiting to see an emergency doctor at my local hospital. Luckily it is within walking distance of my house, so having struggled to get dressed, I had walked there to seek help.

The doctor on duty asked me a few questions, focusing on whether I had suffered a cold or any other type of infection recently. He felt my joints, flexed my arms a bit and said that he thought I was suffering from reactive arthritis, meaning my joints had become painful because of some recent infection of some kind. He gave me a box of strong pain killers and reassured me that it should soon clear up and that I should make an appointment to see my own doctor in the next few days just to make sure. I wasn't particularly worried, even if I was a bit frustrated about missing a bike ride.

Over the next week or so, I suffered constant intense pain. I could barely turn my head, my arms and elbows hurt, even chewing food gave me pain in my jaw. My own doctor agreed with the provisional diagnosis from her colleague at the hospital. She gave me another course of pain killers and said that if the pain persisted when I had completed the course, I should come back and she would consider seeking more specialist help.

Over the next few weeks I learned about what it is like to live with constant pain. I had always thought that arthritis was a kind of nagging, background discomfort. A bit like if you're seated next to someone who is listening to music on headphones. The irritating 'tss tss tss' is annoying, but not insufferable. The pain of arthritis isn't like that at all. It is more like a rock concert taking place in your next door neighbour's garden whilst you're trying to have an afternoon nap. There is no ignoring it, no putting it out of your mind. It becomes a constant part of your life. It seeps into every moment and utterly exhausts you.

I had reached the stage that meant waking up each morning saw me curled in the foetal position, with my fists tightly clenched. This wasn't deliberate – this was something my body was doing by itself. The only way I could get out of bed was to rock myself back and forth until my momentum carried me forward far enough to mean that I was sitting up. I could slowly stand and then creep to the bathroom. My feet where so painful that it felt like I was walking barefoot across a pebbled beach. Even taking a shower was difficult – my hands couldn't grip or squeeze a shampoo bottle and as my body slowly unfurled itself to allow me to wash, every movement was painful.

Gradually as the day progressed, the pain in my joints would ease a bit, which meant I could at least walk around and function at a fairly basic level. I was managing to drive around for my job, but the fact that I was in constant pain left me exhausted. I was so tired on one occasion that I pulled into a lay-by at the side of a busy main road and fell asleep instantly, despite the noise of heavy lorries passing only feet away from where I was parked. This tiredness became a part of my everyday life, along with the handfuls of painkillers that I was taking.

Of course, apart from the pain, there was the fact that cycling was impossible. I don't know if it was because of constant use, being constantly flexed without being put under too much strain, but the only joints that remained unaffected were my hips and my knees. This meant that the action of simply pedalling didn't cause a problem, but as I couldn't hold the handlebars, much less operate brakes or gears, any time out on my bike was utterly out of the question. This made me angry – I had spent the last four years gradually turning myself from a sloth to a reasonably fit man. I had put hours of effort into getting myself fit, then, all of a sudden, the results of all my efforts were slipping away.

The painkillers from my own doctor simply hadn't worked. I saw my health deteriorate at an alarming rate as I waited for a hospital appointment, at which I finally found myself in front of Dr. Andrew Gough, a local rheumatologist.

He was pleasant, understanding and cheerful. He asked plenty of questions, moved my joints about and gently prodded and poked at me whilst talking me through what he was looking for. After he had finished, he explained to me about rheumatoid arthritis, and how I would need some more tests, but that he thought my problems might be related to a family history of psoriasis, which had manifested itself in the form of arthritis in my case, as my body's immune system was attacking my joints, rather than my skin, which was what had happened to my dad in his early thirties.

I saw Dr. Gough again a couple of weeks later. During this time I had continued the daily ritual of slowly unravelling my body each morning, before struggling through the rest of my day, limping from place to place while wishing I could think of something to do to fill the void left by not being able to ride my bike. The trouble was that whatever I thought of was made impossible by my painful joints. I thought about maybe going back to the day my friend Paul Bennett had shown me his electric guitar for the first time, and I had spent the intervening years learning to play, occasionally joining bands and performing in pubs and bars. This was no good – my hands hurt too much and were useless for anything as fiddly as playing guitar. I thought about doing more cooking, something I have always enjoyed and considered myself reasonably good at.

This was no good either – it was hard to feed myself at times, never mind use a knife to chop ingredients or grip a spoon to stir a sauce. The sheer fatigue of the constant pain meant that I filled most of my spare time watching television, barely able to stay awake. For the first time in years, I avoided watching any cycling or reading any cycling magazines, even though the ones I had subscribed to continued to fall through my letterbox. I just couldn't face it; I didn't want to even consider the possibility of having to give up cycling, having come so far.

When I saw Dr. Gough again, he explained that my test results showed that it was likely that I had rheumatoid arthritis. He spoke about treatment options, and also asked me if I would be interested in taking part in a drug trial. As I have worked in the pharmaceutical industry, I knew that this would probably be a good option. I knew it would mean that I would be more closely monitored and would have more chance to see clinicians and hopefully learn more about how I might get better. I agreed to take part. I didn't realise at the time that I had just made a potentially life changing decision.

I was called to see two research nurses called Beverly and Esther. I sat in the waiting room of the McMillan Centre at Harrogate Hospital. I was still feeling pretty sorry for myself – the pain hadn't got any better, I permanently looked tired and haggard and the tablets I was taking had hardly reduced the pain and just made me feel depressed. I looked around at some of the other people who were waiting. I was struck by how many of the women were wearing head-scarves, brightly coloured and closely fitted to their heads. Then I realised that they were probably covering heads made bald from cancer treatments. It put my own condition into sharp perspective and I felt a pang of guilt about the way I worried about my condition. I had pain and couldn't ride my bike. Not good, maybe life changing, but not life threatening.

Beverly and Esther were brilliant. They reassured me, answered all of my questions with patience and understanding and made me feel much less anxious. Up until this point, and despite my reflections in the waiting room about those much worse off than me, I don't think I had quite grasped that I really was quite ill. There was a chance that I would suffer symptoms for years, if not for good and that my life could take a dramatic turn for the worse. There was just one point, as I was having my blood pressure measured whilst answering more questions and having my joints felt, that I briefly considered the worst possible outcome, I was suddenly scared. I managed to hold back tears and then pulled myself together whilst Beverly explained what was planned for me.

I was given a small brown book which recorded all my blood test results. I kept this with me, and brought it to all my appointments from that day on. I was also given a box full of tiny bottles of white powder, some vials of water and a box of needles. Beverly showed me how to draw water from one of the vials, add it to the powder in one of the small bottles, draw the mixture into a needle and inject it under the skin on my stomach. This was to be a weekly ritual for me from then on. I did the first injection there and then in the clinic. I went home feeling glad that at last I was doing something, that things might start to get better from then on.

The next day I woke up as usual, and began the ritual of trying to unravel my body, open up my hands and get myself moving. I was sure that it was easier than it had been for months. I was sure that my hands opened up with less pain and that as I walked around there was less of a feeling of stepping on pebbles. Not quite the feeling of soft carpet and painless progress, but less uncomfortable than I had become used to. I told myself this was simply the placebo effect of having finally started to do something to treat the illness.

Over the coming days there was a definite improvement. Even so, I tried my best not to become too optimistic. I gave myself another injection the next week and a few days later went back to see Beverly. She came into the waiting room to call my name and accompany me down the corridor to her consulting room. The last time I had made this short journey, I couldn't help noticing the concerned look on Beverly's face, and the way she subtly walked at my pace, which was obviously much slower than if she were walking down that same corridor on her own. I can still remember how every step hurt and how Beverly just told me to take it steady and not rush myself too much. This time though, was different. I almost wanted to tell Beverly to try harder to keep up. I hardly had any pain. As I filled in another questionnaire about my symptoms, I realised that the improvement I thought I had felt in the last two weeks was much more than a figment of my imagination or the result of any placebo effect. I was undeniably getting better.

I was back to the stage where I could now function pretty much as I had before. Early mornings no longer meant slowly and carefully easing every joint back to life, I could cut up food, tie my laces and walk almost normally. There was just one thing left, one question that I really wanted to answer, the one thing I wanted to do almost more than anything else. I wondered – could I ride my bike?

Throughout my illness I think I had used a combination of stubbornness and denial as a way of coping with what was happening to me. I had never really contemplated the prospect of long term, chronic illness, and perhaps even a level of disability that would not only put demands on me, but also on those around me. I had just continued doing as many of the things I normally did as I could. I still went out to work every day, even though I had to allow extra time to drive anywhere as well as extra time to ease myself out of the car when I reached my destination. I still went out to the pub occasionally and found that a few pints seemed to mean less pain the following day, I started calling this an 'inverted hangover'. I looked terrible, was in pain, but tried to carry on almost as normal, except of course for one thing. The one thing I wanted to do as much as, if not more than, anything else.

Now though, I had been lucky. The day when I had said 'yes' to the drug trial had changed the journey I was on, it had put me in a place that had been potentially unreachable only months ago.

It was a pleasant evening, and I had finished work for the day, had something to eat and was sitting on my patio enjoying a pleasant summer's evening. I had been contemplating that final step back to what I considered to be full recovery. I felt that if I could manage to ride my bike without too much discomfort, I would be able to consider myself to be truly over the worst. I sat and held my arms out in front of me. My hands were parallel to each other, unlike the twisted, deviated way they were only weeks before. I flexed my shoulders, and curled my toes. No pain. I clenched both my fists and looked at the way the creases in my fingers meant there were no gaps, or light showing through. Up until recently I could barely bend my fingers at all. Then I went upstairs to my office, and took my bike down from its hanger on the wall for the first time in months. I sat on the saddle, squeezed the brake levers and clicked the gears. It felt almost the same as it always had. Then I carried it downstairs, took it into the garden and pumped up the tyres. All was ready.

Not wanting to be over ambitious, pretty much in the same way as when I had first ridden the bike I bought from Halfords when I started cycling again, I decided on a short circuit, just to see how I felt. As I wound my way out of the clutches of the town centre, with its traffic lights and junctions, I was able to start riding properly, unrestricted by anything other than my own efforts. I rode uphill for a while, just enjoying the feeling of pushing hard on the pedals again, before sweeping down a road that I had ridden many times before. I bounced over a few potholes, and felt nothing more than the usual jarring sensation. My hands didn't hurt, and my back and shoulders felt relaxed and comfortable. Another short climb meant I emerged from a line of trees to a view across open fields and moors lit by the golden light of the evening sun. On any summers day or night this would have been a pleasure, but this time I enjoyed that view more than I ever had before.

As I rolled back toward home, taking in the sights and sounds of what was around me, I realised just how good some of the things we take for granted really are. I had ridden those roads hundreds of times and had stopped noticing how nice they were. I had come close to losing all of this and much more.

I no longer considered myself 'ill', I had been lucky enough to meet a team of people who had made me well again. The true definition of being well is so much more than 'an absence of illness', and this bike ride was my own personal way of showing myself that things had turned out well. I have never been so thankful for the chance to have an hour on my bike as I was on that evening. In a way, it meant the bicycle, a symbol of so much freedom to so many people across the world had reminded me that it too gave me freedom. I was free of symptoms, free of pain and free to be very happy.

From then on I was able to ride regularly and couldn't help noticing the irony of the fact that I was a cyclist with a fridge full of drugs and syringes that I used regularly to help me perform better. Thankfully, my recovery continued and the following spring I was no longer injecting myself and was discussing with Dr. Gough about stopping the last of my medications. I had entered the Etape du Tour again as a way of finally declaring myself back to where I wanted to be and didn't want to jeopardise my fitness for the sake of stopping taking a couple of tablets a week. We agreed the best thing would be to wait until after the Etape for me to become treatment free.

In July, Paul and I set off for France once more, in the company of our Red Kite club mates and we rode to the top of Mont Ventoux. It was a fantastic day, ending on an iconic mountain. There were hundreds of people at the finish when I crossed the line, taking photos of themselves' alongside the famous observatory that I had seen on television so many times as the professionals struggled towards it.

Everyone was pleased to be there, thankful that they had the opportunity to fulfil dreams and emulate their heroes. I like to think, that having nearly lost the chance to ride a bike again, I was amongst the most thankful of all.

Stage 12
Join our Club

Despite the fact that human beings are, generally speaking, hard wired to be sociable, there are times when a bit of solitude can be a pleasure. With a busy work and family life, the opportunity to spend a bit of selfish 'me time' was fairly limited to me, but riding my bike often became a good opportunity to spend a bit of time on my own without actually looking like I was being too anti-social. I was beginning to quite enjoy my solo bike rides. There is certainly something quite wonderful about being on a desolate moorland road, knowing that you are the only person for miles around.

The trouble is that solo cycling has also some disadvantages. There is no one to draft behind to get a bit of shelter from the wind, no one to chat to if you stop for a coffee or if you actually feel like a chat when you're riding along. Then there is the fact that your knowledge of nice routes is limited to those you discover yourself. If something goes wrong, there is no one to help with an awkwardly twisted chain, or to add a bit of extra air to re-inflate a punctured tyre. And a group is more visible, therefore much safer, than someone riding alone.

Above all though, most pastimes are more fun with someone else. It had been amazing to be part of an event as huge as the Etape du Tour; to be part of a mass of eight thousand cyclists all riding the same route. I had felt envious of people I had seen who were riding together in groups, often in matching kit. I even saw someone from Hull Thursday Road Club, which set me thinking about joining a cycling club again, and perhaps getting even more committed to riding my bike.

Later that year, I noticed in the cycling press that one of the local cycling clubs was staging its end of season hill climb on Norwood Edge, so I thought it might be a nice way to spend a morning and even managed to persuade two of my sons to come with me. I also thought it would be a chance to ask about joining one of the local clubs, as they would all be represented.

Norwood Edge is a hill that plays an ever present role in my life as a cyclist and in the lives of many cyclists who live near to me. It starts as the road crosses a dam at the end of a reservoir and then rises up steeply through some trees. The surface is quite cut up and rough. It's steep enough to send me searching for my lowest gear, and to have me out of the saddle and out of breath very quickly. The road turns to the right and begins to level out a bit, at least giving me the chance to sit back in the saddle and get my breath back. It then cuts a graceful sweep to the left and steepens once again, before undulating towards its peak in a wood, with a view of a wind farm and an American spy base that finally confirms that the climb is over. I must have climbed it hundreds of times over the years. Its close enough to my home to be included as part of a short ride when I need a few quality miles and can't afford the time to have the luxury of quantity. At other times as we approach home after a long day of riding, someone in the group will decide, either because of bravado or the need for a bit of extra 'hill training', that they want us to turn and climb it, instead of cruising home along flatter roads.

When my sons and I got to Norwood Edge on the day of the hill climb, they seemed more interested in the wrecked car that the low water level in the reservoir had exposed than they were in watching cyclists struggle up the hill. We walked along the side of the road, watching riders go past us at a speed that varied from very impressive to just above walking pace. There were a few other people watching and I saw one lady dressed in a cycling jersey of one of the local clubs. I approached and asked her if they held regular club runs, as I was keen to start cycling properly again.

'They do have club runs but they're a bit of a sore point' said the woman. 'They always end up arguing. New people come along and can't keep up so they never come back or everyone waits for them but moans so much that the outcome is the same, they never come back. Or they just argue because some of them want to go fast and some of them want to go easy and stop for a cup of tea'.

It all sounded so familiar. Those club runs that Dicco and I so enjoyed suffered the same problems. We'd be happily cruising along in our replica team jerseys, dreaming of our future Tour de France glories and trying to go as fast as we could, often sprinting to beat each other past village signs or staging our own little breakaways from the group. This often wasn't a problem, because many of the runs we went on were organised by a man called Arthur who had been a pretty decent racer in his younger days, and he seemed to enjoy seeing our enthusiasm. However, there seemed to be another group of club members who'd occasionally come on our club runs and start complaining if we went above ten miles an hour. They'd moan about the speed we were going, moan about the fact that we never had mudguards on our bikes, moan that we were wearing replica team jerseys ('They're a bloody con – those companies must be laughing all the way to the bloody bank'). They seemed to hate the fact that we favoured modern equipment and they held firmly of the opinion that anything that had been invented in the last twenty years was rubbish that served no other purpose than to make them spend money they would rather keep.

I suppose I shouldn't have been surprised that in the world of cycling these attitudes seemed to have remained. Even today, on any Sunday there must be countless cycling clubs riding around the countryside arguing about how fast or slow they are going, about equipment, about just about everything, then complaining that membership was down this year yet again.

Having decided that I didn't want to risk causing yet more arguments in a cycling club that were perfectly happy arguing amongst themselves, I thought it would be good to try to set up a group with a few of the people with whom I'd ridden before.

After I had done the Etape du Tour, I was beginning to feel that I'd be able to contribute something to a group of relative newcomers to the sport who wanted to start riding together. There had been a few of us who had met up to make the original trip and we had stayed in contact with each other. We had started to occasionally meet up for rides, usually setting off from outside the Minster in York. As I'd already decided that I couldn't possibly turn down the chance to ride up the famous Alpe d'Huez climb in the next Etape, a regular group ride was just what I needed to make me get out of bed on the sort of grey winter's morning when a lie in and a bacon sandwich was a much more appealing prospect than a bike ride.

Gradually, through word of mouth and an ever increasing chain of e-mails, we began to evolve into a more formal group. A few of us began to enter some local events, many of which asked for you to say which group or club you were part of. It seemed a natural thing for us all to put the same club name on our entries, so that we would be able to ride together.

Bearing in mind the inverse relationship between the amount of money we had all spent on equipment, and the lack of natural cycling talent, we considered 'All the gear, No idea', but this was quickly dismissed, because it felt like too much of a mouthful to say, and usually too long to fit in the space on many event entry forms. We wanted something that didn't sound too grand and that was inclusive enough for us all.

One of the many iconic images in cycling is that of the 'Flamme Rouge'. This is a little red banner that is always suspended over the road to mark the point where the riders in a race enter the last kilometre. However, a group of middle aged men wearing Lycra and calling themselves 'Flamme Rouge' seemed more likely to conjure up images of some kind of transvestite cross-dressing society, rather than a cycling club. In English though, the 'Flamme Rouge' is called the 'Red Kite'. In addition to this, near where I live, there is a breeding program for red kites. It has been so successful that these birds are a common sight. The joint meaning of something that had become a bit of a local symbol, it also had a meaningful place in the world of cycling so seemed to make the perfect choice, our group became known as 'Red Kite'.

The great thing about this set up was that because we were simply a group of like-minded friends who had agreed to meet up once a month to go for a ride, we had all the advantages of being in a club, with none of the disadvantages. The advantages of course being that our monthly rides were pretty sociable affairs. We would agree on an end point and set off in a pretty disorganised two abreast formation, chatting happily and enjoying the day. The only thing approaching a rule that we had was that we waited for each other at the top of every hill and at road junctions. This should have meant that we spent most of the time riding as a group and that no one ever got lost. In reality it meant that there would be frequent occasions when someone would shoot past a road junction in which we were all waiting, and we would spend half the day chasing each other or trying unsuccessfully to get a decent phone signal to re-direct some errant member of the group back to our original course. Thankfully we would always have some particular cafe or tea room in mind as a rest stop, so even if we had all ended up going in different directions for much of the day, we usually managed to at least have a cup of tea and a cake together.

One we thing we noticed on our monthly rides was the ever increasing number of cyclists on the road, many of whom were in groups of their own. They all seemed to look better than us. This may have been due to the fact that they had been cycling for years, and could easily ride in a group without frightening each other, and always seemed able to stay together up hills and between road junctions. It could have been their well-maintained bikes and their natural pedalling style. But what really stood out, and really made us envious, was the fact that some of these groups were wearing matching jerseys. We realised that even though we would never be quite such smooth pedalling and elite looking cyclists as most of the other groups we saw, we could at least try and look the part by all buying some matching Lycra.

It's very easy these days to let your imagination run wild when you're designing a cycling jersey. The jerseys Dicco and I used to wear relied on sewn on lettering and embroidery for their designs. This not only limited what could be done, but also made them very expensive and labour intensive to produce. Modern jerseys are printed, so anything is possible. You can buy designs based on anything from wine labels to Tunnock's biscuit boxes, and even the label from a jar of Marmite, a design of jersey that some people love and naturally some people hate.

I had a play around on my computer and came up with a design based on the colours of Bradford City FC, as I have spent many rainy afternoons on the terraces of Valley Parade. I didn't actually tell anyone the reasons for the colour scheme, but everyone seemed happy enough so the jerseys were ordered and once they arrived, I met my club mates outside York Minster to set off on our first club run in our new outfits. It was a chilly winter's day, but the sun was out and we felt quite proud of ourselves as we left the city. A couple of other riders who were visiting York for the weekend had joined us, one of whom was a lady who worked for British Cycling. They had actually been hoping to meet up with a different club, but once they'd seen the 'Red Kites' they must have been impressed enough to join us instead.

There are times in life when old sayings come true, sometimes in an alarming way. As we were cycling through the countryside I felt a sense of pride in the way we looked. I felt this sense of pride just before I unknowingly led the group down a road covered in black ice. One minute I was happily chatting to someone, the next I was part of a tangled heap of bikes and middle aged men trying to stand up on a slippery surface whilst wearing cycling shoes and trying to untangle themselves from their bikes and each other.

Those who had managed to avoid the fall were stopped a few metres up the road. As they tried not to laugh too much at what had just happened, two of them also slipped on the ice, which was much more extensive than we had realised. It was so slippery that we had to walk along the grass verge until we reached a patch of dry road before setting off on a short cut home to compare bruises and comfort ourselves with tea and cake.

Despite this inauspicious start, we rode as a club regularly and took part in events all over the North. Over the years there were Red Kite jerseys present at a few editions of the Etape du Tour (including a special one based on Tommy Simpson's iconic Peugeot jersey when we all rode up Mont Ventoux). We even got to the point where we didn't lose each other on club runs, could ride fairly comfortably and safely as a group and actually looked like we knew what we were doing to other cyclists passing from the other direction.

Although we never grew beyond a couple of dozen regulars we functioned quite well as a club, enjoyed some great rides and even a trip to try out the track in Manchester. The club only lasted a couple of years – but it was the family and work commitments of everyone involved which led to it petering out, rather than arguments about not letting people keep up, about going too fast, or where to stop for cups of tea. It is almost as if we were too like-minded and the mixture of clashing personalities that make up most clubs wasn't really there, a bit like a recipe with a few ingredients missing. So once again, I had become a solo cyclist, occasionally riding with Paul, but mostly I was on my own.

Again, I started to miss group riding and the friendship a club can offer. One day, I was browsing on the internet when I came across a website for the Cappuccino Cycling Club, which was based in Harrogate.

The club had been started by James Lovell and the description on the website made it sound like just what I needed. It said that they aimed to enjoy cycling and that the club runs would always include somewhere to stop for coffee and cake. Even though it made no mention of these refreshment stops including pork pies, I decided to get in touch.

As with my days as a youngster in Hull Thursday, the club had its own cast of characters made up of the sort of people who always seem to join a cycling club. There are always a few friendly faces, a few people obsessed with equipment (and talking about it), and a least one dour older member who seems unfriendly and as if he only comes out on a Sunday in order to have the opportunity to complain about things and find someone new to shout at. Every club has someone like this, and what many people don't realise is that they are usually an asset to the club, because they often have a heart of gold, without them the type of disorganised chaos that my early rides with the Red Kites used to descend into becomes the norm. This usually leads to more arguments and falling out. Also, these seemingly gruff men usually have a lot of knowledge and experience and if others can see through their harsh exterior, they can help everyone else learn a lot.

The vast majority of the older club men were like this back in the nineteen-seventies, often modelling their behaviour on the sort of men who used to teach us PE in school or had shouted at them when they were doing their national service, seemingly enjoying seeing us suffer whilst passing their time in relative comfort.

I was a regular on winter club runs as a young member of Hull Thursday, and was surprised to see an unusually high turn out on the day of the 'Presidents Run'. A huge group of us rode out across the Plain of Holderness, east of Hull, towards the seaside town of Withernsea. It was cold and there was a biting headwind, by the time it was my turn to ride at the front I was both frozen and tired. I could feel the strength draining from my legs and was terrified of looking like I couldn't cope. No matter how hard I tried, every pedal stroke was painful. Being only about thirteen years old, I felt I had to wait for permission to move off the front and have a break at the back of the long line of riders and by time this was granted by the senior club member alongside me, I was close to tears. When we finally got to the pub where we were stopping and began to unwrap our packed lunches, I was shattered. The mystery of the huge turnout was solved when the president bought a drink for everyone, before he came over to me and said, 'You looked to be struggling a bit then Martin'.

'I was', I admitted, 'it was hard'.

'We just thought it would do you good to leave you out there for a bit', he replied, before going off to sit with someone closer to his own age.

It was a chap called Malcolm who had adopted this type of philosophy amongst those riding on the regular Cappuccino club rides. Despite his gruff exterior he knew a lot and shared his years of experience with everyone else, whether they wanted him to or not. The result of this of course, was that everyone learned a lot from him. One of the nicest routes out of Harrogate passes a cemetery on the moors towards Wharfedale. It's a very windswept and barren place and Malcolm always said that it was where he wanted his ashes scattered, having been carried there by members of the club. He added to his wish by hoping that on the day there would be 'a bloody great headwind'.

One problem with a group of people meeting to go on a bike ride is that often no one wants to take the initiative and decide where to go. The ability to make a decision seems to decline once there are more than about half a dozen people involved in the decision making process. What is really needed is someone with a vast knowledge of local roads, gained through experience of thousands of miles of riding over the years. Thankfully, a man called Martin Procter fitted the bill perfectly and he became a regular on Cappuccino club rides, so he found himself appointed as default ride leader.

Thinking back, I could remember people in Hull Thursday Road Club all those years ago who fulfilled similar roles and characters among them: 'ex top local racer man' (noticeable by general cynicism of anyone currently racing at any level) and the inevitable 'new kit man' (noticeable for having lots of shiny new kit, which he attempts to justify by arguing that it is worth spending several hundred pounds to save the equivalent weight of a decent pre-ride bowel movement). All this meant that I very quickly felt at home, and I was soon riding with the 'Cappos' as often as I could.

Over the first year or so, the club grew and grew. The next step in its development was getting some matching kit for everyone. James came up with a very stylish design and in a similar piece of subterfuge to me making everyone in the Red Kite club wear Bradford City colours, he based it on the colours of the flag of his native Cornwall. Luckily, black, white and gold is a good combination, so the jerseys looked very smart.

Once the club had become more established, we decided to start riding some local events, one of the biggest of which is the Great Yorkshire Bike Ride which is held every year and runs for about seventy miles from the market town of Wetherby to the seaside resort of Filey.

This was promising to be the first really big day out for the club, as we would all have our new jerseys and would be riding in a big event along with hundreds of other cyclists of all ages and abilities. If people saw us, it might prove a good way to get a few more members. The prospect of a good day turning into a great one was made possible when one of the regular riders, Karl, offered to help with getting us all back to Harrogate. Karl's family business supplies buses and coaches. Karl said he could lend us one for the day and that the driver would even stop at a pub on the way back if we wanted. It began to look like we were going to have the perfect combination of a nice long bike ride and a traditional English day at the seaside.

In the true spirit of a traditional English day at the seaside, the weather was wet and miserable, but no one let it dampen spirits. We had all left our bags at Karl's house, ready to be transported to the finish by our coach driver. The riders were being allowed to set off in groups of about thirty, which meant that our group got to set off as one, all resplendent in our new club jerseys.

We had obviously been paying some attention to the 'advice' that Malcolm had shared with us over the last few months, because we managed to ride along at a decent pace, sharing time at the front of the group while generally giving the impression that we really knew what we were doing, at least in the eyes of many of the participants who were probably doing their only ride of the year. This impression was reinforced in our own minds as we approached the end of the ride.

Karl had told us that the coach would be in the car park by the finish and that we would easily recognise it because he would have put some Cappuccino Cycling Club stickers on it. When we spotted it, we could hardly believe our eyes – it wasn't just decked out with a few stickers, but had been painted with full Cappuccino Cycling Club livery. It had the club name down both sides along with the web site address, and 'Cappuccino Cycling Club' written under the windscreen at the right level to appear in the rear view mirror of any car that passed it.

Everyone was so delighted with the coach that we took turns having our picture taken in front of it, then loading our bikes into the space that had been created in the back by taking out some of the seats.

With our bags on board it meant we could all change out of our damp new club kit into dry, comfortable clothes for the trip to the pub that was planned as a break on the journey home. As we pulled out of the car park we waved at some of the people who were waiting for their own transport home and who looked unsure whether to think we were the most impressive club they had ever come across or the biggest bunch of show-offs, who they sincerely hoped would have to push their flashy private coach home after it had broken down. Thankfully, we didn't suffer this indignity and even Malcolm said how much he had enjoyed the event, just as he drained his third pint in the pub on the way home.

As we sat reflecting on our day, I had the feeling that I had found a lot of the things I had been looking for since I started cycling again.

It had been a few years since I had stood in my local branch of Halfords, looking at a cheap alloy bike, buying it and setting off on my first tentative rides. I had tried to recapture my youth and the happy days Dicco and I spent on our bikes. I looked around the smiling group of friends, draining their glasses and talking again about different parts of a brilliant day.

I was back in a cycling club, with new friends, regular club runs, and the things that being in a cycling club can add to life as a cyclist; it felt like the last piece of the jigsaw was in place. It is a place where people disagree about how fast we should go, about what a waste of money new equipment is, about people who turn up on rainy days without fitting mudguards and which café serves the best pork pies. It is a fully functioning, living, breathing, cycling club.

Grim Up North

There can be little doubt that the Tour de France is very much the glamorous side of cycling. It has the highest profile of any race in the world; all the sport's stars want to be seen there, along with anyone else who has any part to play, however small. It has sunshine, beautiful people, beautiful scenery, heroes and villains, and nearly always a happy ending. It's the Hollywood of cycling with the paparazzi to match.

But just like the world of films, cycling has another, tougher, side. Many of the world's greatest actors never go to Hollywood and some of the finest performances ever captured on camera have taken place miles away from the glamour of 'tinsel town'. These are those types of 'gritty dramas' that set good men against bad and strong women against the world. They usually have the sort of story-line where the heroine is downtrodden but beautiful, the sort of woman who has to put up with abuse and neglect, heartbreak and tragedy, where the best people don't always come out on top. Not because they do anything wrong, or turn out to be weak in some way, but because life has a habit of robbing the good in what often seems like the bitterest twist of fate.

Cycling's 'gritty dramas' take place each year, in a series of races known as the 'Spring classics'. To attain the status of a 'classic' a race has to have a few basic, if somewhat undefined elements. It has to be long – often over two hundred kilometres, it has to be tough and it has to have been run for a long time preferably over roads as old as the race itself.

These races though, aren't without their share of glamour and beauty. They start with the Milan – San Remo, known as 'la primevera'. Riders leave the outskirts of Milan and race to the Mediterranean coast, usually finishing in a huge bunch sprint under sunny skies. It's seen as the start of the season proper, and has cycling fans across Europe looking forward to warmer weather and nicer rides on their best summer bikes. For many, it heralds the start of spring.

Then, just as the characters in the new season's story start to develop their sun tans, the whole of the cycling circus moves northwards, to the fields of Northern France and Flanders. This is when the 'gritty drama' starts to unfold. This is when the cobbled classics take place. The three most famous of these being the Tour of Flanders, the Liege-Bastogne-Liege and the Paris-Roubaix. These three races are as old as the sport of cycling itself and all have produced heroes throughout the years who have as much right to their place in cycling's hall of fame as any of the winners of the Tour de France.

They take place against a back drop of grim industrial landscapes and charming medieval towns. There are no great mountain passes to be crossed and no majestic alpine scenery. The races are sometimes hilly but the climbs are short and vicious rather than the long hours of uphill suffering that awaits the riders in the Tour de France each July. Usually, these short climbs come in quick succession, often after many kilometres of racing in wind and rain on muddy roads. Many of these climbs are as famous as some of the great passes of the Alps and Pyrenees.

The hill known as the Koppenberg, which makes up part of the Tour of Flanders, is only six hundred metres long – so short that it probably wouldn't even register as a climb in some races, but on its steepest section the gradient is twenty-two per cent, more than one in five. Add to this the fact the surface is made up of cobbles that are often wet on race day, and that the road is barely two metres wide, it doesn't take much imagination to see why it can have such an effect on the outcome of the race. It is just as much of a shrine to cyclists as Mont Ventoux or Alpe D'Huez.

The Liege-Bastogne-Liege is the oldest of the classics, and is known as 'la Doyenne ('The old Lady)'. It was first run in 1892, when the winning rider, a local man called Leon Houa took eleven hours to complete the course. It is also usually one of the longest races that the professional riders face each year and is hard all the way to finish. One of its most fabled climbs is called La Redoute and the organisers usually make sure it comes right at the end, after the riders have been racing for 220 kilometres. It is as steep as fifteen per cent (or one in six) at its hardest part. To win the race you need to attack this hill harder than your rivals, even with all those miles of tough racing and relentless climbs in your legs. It is a true test of stamina and of having the tactical sense to conserve energy until exactly the right moment.

The great French rider Bernard Hinault created one of the great stories of modern cycling when he rode the 1980 edition of the race. Not long before the start, heavy snow began to fall, combined with strong winds. Many riders had realised how bad the weather was going to be and did not even take the start. As the day went on, riders dropped out dozens at a time. At one point Hinault decided to join them but his team mate, Maurice Le Guillox, persuaded him to ride on as far as the first feed station. The two of them went back to their team car to ask for dry gloves. The team manager, Cyrille Guimard wasn't impressed. Sitting in his nice warm car, much in the same way as my PE teachers used to watch me try to play rugby in a blizzard, whilst they drank hot coffee and kept warm in a sheepskin coat, he actually told Hinault to take his waterproof jacket off 'because the real racing is about to start'. The only thing Hinault could do was ride as hard as he could as a way of keeping warm. He rode so hard that he passed the two riders who had broken away from the peloton, and simply kept going all the way to the finish. Spectators by the roadside were wearing goggles to help them peer through the murkiness to see the riders pass. Hinault was entirely alone and ploughed on to win by over nine minutes, ahead of second placed Hennie Kuiper. As he rode down the finish straight he passed the hotel where the majority of riders who had abandoned the race were warming themselves in comfort and as he saw them by the roadside, he saluted to them. Of the 174 riders who took the start, only 21 of them finished, the last man being nearly half an hour behind Hinault. Thankfully, most of Hinault's team mates had got themselves back to the team hotel and, having had a nice bath, were watching the race on television. They were ready to help him thaw out, but it was weeks before the feeling returned to Hinault's frozen fingers, and he has suffered problems with them ever since.

Aside from the high chance of bad weather, it is the roads that make up the routes of the classics that add so much to the story and make these races so famous in the world of cycling. Throughout their history, organisers have sought out rough cobbled roads to challenge the riders. There are plenty of these to choose from in Northern France and even though modern tarmac is used more and more, the old farm tracks are used so rarely that they are in much the same state now as they were a hundred years ago when the races were first run.

As well as 'La doyenne' and the Tour of Flanders, there is also 'the Queen of the Classics', probably the most legendary race of all - the Paris Roubaix. It invokes fear and respect in equal measure, hence its other name, 'The Hell of the North'.

What makes the race so famous, and gives it its reputation for toughness, is that the route is deliberately designed to take in the worst roads possible. These mostly consist of ancient cobbled farm tracks, which were built to withstand years of abuse from heavy agricultural machinery, rather than skinny men on lightweight bikes. There is even an organisation dedicated to preserving these roads and protecting them from the risk of being resurfaced in tarmac. Because it is run in early April, around the same time as Liege-Bastogne-Liege, once again the weather tends to be cold, wet and windy, and even the well surfaced parts of the course tend to be muddy and slippery. The final part of the race takes riders into the outskirts of Roubaix before riding into the town's outdoor velodrome to cross the finish line. The velodrome itself has become something of a shrine in the world of cycling.

It has a huge sculpture of a cobblestone by the entrance, and each of its primitive shower cubicles are decorated with a plaque commemorating a famous past winner. Winners of Paris-Roubaix don't just get a commemorative shower cubicle though, winning in the Roubaix velodrome gives a rider his place amongst the greats in the history of the sport. Many riders who have never featured in the results of the Tour de France built their reputations on winning it. Years ago, riders like Bernard Hinault could win both the Tour de France and races like the Paris-Roubaix, but as the sport has evolved, with riders and teams focusing on specific objectives, those days seem to be over. In the modern era, riders seem to either become grand tour contenders, or 'classics men'. Hollywood or art house.

Dicco and I hadn't made our 'classics or grand tour' choice at the time we used to ride our bikes around East Yorkshire. The terrain in that part of the world is often quite flat and in the early part of the year farmers would plough their fields ready for sowing their crops and the landscape would take on a bleak and brown appearance. The weather meant that there would often be a lot of mud washed onto the roads, which were in pretty poor condition anyway, with potholes and broken tarmac almost everywhere. In our schoolboy minds, this was exactly like the scenery of Northern France and Flanders, across which our heroes were racing. If only there had been a way we could have found to ride over miles of cobbles, our happiness would have been truly complete.

Having fulfilled one part of my dreams when I'd ridden a stage of the Tour de France by completing the Etape, I had a vague feeling that I wanted to experience one of the classics as well, to make me feel like a 'complete rider', just like the greats of old, at least in my own mind.

Whilst working at my computer one day, an e mail popped into my in-box, from ASO, the organisers of the Etape I had ridden. It was a survey which promised the chance to win a bike if you completed it. It asked a lot of questions about whether or not I'd be interested in having the chance to ride an Etape-style event that followed the route of one of the spring classic races. I ticked yes, and sent my answers off, then waited for the delivery of the first prize of a nice new bike. Sadly I didn't win, but a few months later ASO e-mailed again to say that they were going ahead with their idea of allowing middle-aged dreamers like me to ride the Paris-Roubaix route on closed roads, with the finish in the famous velodrome at Roubaix.

This was about the same time that my wife had decided that her life would be better without me being part of it, so I had become a part-time bachelor and part-time parent, leaving me with something of a gap in my life. I was feeling that I deserved a treat to cheer myself up, so I decided to enter. Paul had already persuaded me that doing the Etape du Tour yet again would be a good form of diversionary therapy and I even convinced myself, (and anyone else who would listen) that it gave my 'season' a profile like a real pro – a spring classic to aim for before changing my training a bit and getting ready for the Alps in summer. I tried to convince some friends from my club to join me and although a few of them seemed keen, by the time I had paid my deposit to a tour company, I had more or less accepted that I would be going on my own. Then a friend, Richard, who I knew through my work said that he and his brother were keen, meaning that I'd have some familiar company for the trip to northern France.

I spent the winter trying to find bits of cobbled road to ride over, much to the amusement of my club mates. Each time I went out I'd ride along the edge of the road, trying to imagine what it was going to be like on the way to Roubaix. I'm sure it didn't help my preparation, but it kept me amused as I steadily built up my mileage.

The trip started with a coach that we had arranged to meet at five thirty in the morning in the centre of Leeds. It was still dark as I stood waiting to meet Richard. The queue must have made a strange site to any onlookers – made up as it was of a bunch of skinny middle aged men talking about cycling and an equal number of peroxide blond Eastern European women who seemed to have just finished a shift working as lap-dancers.

The coach journey was relaxing – there were plenty of seats so it was easy to keep comfortable and getting on the ferry reminded me of the excitement of going on holidays to France as a child. We arrived at our hotel ready for everyone to put their bikes together. I'd decided to rent a bike. I'd justified this by the fact that the rental was about the same price as the new tyres and handlebar tape that my own bike would need after riding over the muddy cobbles to Roubaix, and also thinking that there was a reasonable chance that my bike might get smashed up if I had a heavy fall. It would feel much better picking up bits of someone else's broken carbon bike frame than my own. Luckily, the bike I was given didn't even need its saddle adjusting, so once I'd fitted my pedals I was ready for the group's organised warm up ride.

Before our warm-up, we had to go and sign on for the event itself. When we were given our numbers, we realised that we'd be in the last group allowed to start. Richard was unimpressed with this, so used his fluent French to get us different numbers and we found that we would be starting in the second group, much nearer to the front. We went back to the hotel, enjoyed a pleasant hour riding around the local roads with the group then settled down for dinner and an early night ahead of a very early start on the day of the race. I employed my usual tactic of sampling a couple of local beers to help me sleep. As we sat in the hotel restaurant, the room filled up with local Gendarmes who seemed to enjoy a very leisurely supper before going out for the evening to fight local crime.

We were up early and once again I was reminded of the fact that five o'clock in the morning is not the ideal time to be stuffing yourself with bread, cereal and pancakes, but a forty mile coach trip to arrive in St Quentin for the 7.30 am start didn't really give us much option. By the time we set off, the thermometer was telling us that it was four degrees centigrade but the forecast was promising blue skies and warmer conditions for later in the day. I passed the time on the coach trip eating a bit more, dozing a little and watching the sky gradually start to lighten. I was also wondering what to wear, as although riding on closed roads gives something of a professional experience, there are no team cars to discard clothing as the day warms up. It was cold as we got off the coach, but I didn't want to get uncomfortable later in the day.

We arrived at the start about twenty minutes before the first group was going to be released. Gendarmes were unloading motocross bikes from trailers, and riding them around the start area, standing on the footrests and revving the engines. If the cheesy music blaring over the PA hadn't already woken up the whole neighbourhood, then the fine servants of law and order would surely wake up anyone who was still sleeping.

Richard and I made our way to our allocated start pen, in our new faster group. I began to wonder if trying to get this 'upgrade' was such a good idea. We were surrounded by lots of young looking riders, with matching team jerseys, matched to their expensive looking matching team bikes. I also realised that everyone else seemed to have shaved their legs. I couldn't help feeling that our bravado had left me a little bit out of my depth. I got over this by trying to look as relaxed and confident as I could. Before setting off on the trip I had come up with what I thought was a fail-safe and fairly clever tactical plan. I would simply try to spot a fat Belgian and slipstream him for as long as I could. This would mean I could take advantage of his extensive local knowledge while using his size to provide me with decent shelter from wind and rain. I was struggling to put this idea into operation because there were no fat Belgians in this group, just skinny, fit club riders, who looked like they rode at a fairly high standard.

This feeling was reinforced as soon as we started. There was no gentle warm up, no taking it easy just to get your legs going. The speed was high right from the second we crossed the line. Despite a lack of fat Belgians I did manage to use the slipstream of other riders to help me along.

As we left town the roads opened up a bit, and I found I could move around the group reasonably well. After about ten kilometres, there was a slight rise in the road, as the group slowed a bit, I found myself getting nearer and nearer the front. I drew up alongside Richard and just said, 'I'm having a bit of this'. I moved up and up the line until I found myself on the front of the group. I just put my head down and pedalled as hard as I could. It was an amazing feeling – ahead of me there was an empty road, two motorbikes and a French sunrise, behind me a 300 strong peloton, all strung out because they were keeping to the pace I was setting. Yet again, I found myself thinking that it was probably the best moment I'd ever had on a bike.

The speed stayed high, but I found that I could stay in the top twenty or so riders without too much trouble, just riding in the wheels of others, sometimes closing gaps as they appeared. We passed a sign saying that we had already covered twenty kilometres, and when I looked at my watch, we'd been going for thirty two minutes. I felt fantastic, as if the training had actually been worthwhile, because going this fast wasn't just exciting. I was actually finding it quite easy.

After few more kilometres on rolling roads, and a crazy average speed we arrived in a village called Troisville. As I passed the village sign, something stirred in my memory. I knew this name held some vague significance but I couldn't quite remember why. Then, as we rounded a bend, there was a small sign planted in the side of the road telling us we were about to enter the first sections of *pave* – the cobbles that make these roads so famous. Troisville is the start of the cobbles, and that's why I'd heard of it. This was what I had come for.

Nothing, but nothing, can describe the bumping, jarring shaking sensation of hitting the cobbles. It's almost impossible to hold the handlebars properly, and even the noise is almost deafening as every part of your bike seems as if it's about to shake itself to bits. Looking around is difficult, changing gear almost impossible. In the dry, like it was on the day I rode, you can at least ride down some of the gutters at the side, but you need to be careful because of the huge potholes. The other option is to ride straight down the middle, on the crown of the road, where the stones haven't been quite so badly damaged by farm traffic. This is what the professionals try to do, because they can maintain more of their speed. The difficulty with this is that you have to have a huge amount of speed to maintain, which as an over aged amateur, I just didn't have. I felt my bike slowing as the bumps seemed to eat up every ounce of energy that I was pushing through the pedals. I decided that the gutter would suit me better but then became aware of another disadvantage of this idea. Just like when you join one long queue in a supermarket and you notice that all the other queues seem to be moving faster than the one you have chosen, the other gutter always looks better that the one you're in, so you spend half your time switching sides and having to get across the cobbles.

All the sections were marked at the start to say how long they are, so at least I had some idea of what was ahead. At the end of the first section, the 300 strong group I was in had completely disintegrated, but there were enough riders around me to get into a fair sized group and keep up a decent speed. It was a relief to be back on proper tarmac but I was also looking forward to the next cobbled section.

This was how the ride continued – every time I got back onto smooth tarmac I seemed to be able to join another group of riders who seemed to want to work together quite well and I started to notice that I was seeing the same people time after time. Each section of pave broke groups up, but there was always another group to join. There wasn't much talking but lots of nods of encouragement and signals to warn of hazards.

Then, on a fast straight bit of road when I was in a group of about fifteen riders, someone shouted 'Arenberg, Arenberg'. I looked ahead, and could see a long avenue of high trees with a huge gantry high above. I recognised it from hundreds of old cycling magazines and films – one of the most famous bits of road in the history of cycling – the Arenberg forest. Everyone in the group looked at each other nervously, and the chap to my right, on a very nice old fashioned steel bike told me it was best to try to stay to the right, because the road was better there.

Hitting the cobbles here made everything that had gone before seem easy. It was as if someone had laid a dry stone wall flat, and called it a road. I'm sure it's a lovely place for a bike ride, as there's even a nice cycle path down one side, which the organisers had thoughtfully cordoned off to ensure the authenticity of our experience. I rode some of it in the gutter, and some of it on the cobbles. Much of the verge at the side was so chewed up that there was no way you could ride on it as a way of finding some relief. I was really starting to enjoy myself, spending some time on the crown of the road and some in the gutter when it looked smoother. I saw a sign saying that one of the photographers taking souvenir photographs was just ahead, so I made sure I was in the middle of the cobbles as he took my picture – I wanted the best memory possible. There was quite a bit of celebrating at the end of the Arenberg and a few of the riders in the group I was with gave each other slaps on the back and handshakes as we moved onto the nice tarmac of the modern road. I almost wanted to go back and do the Arenberg again, because it's such an iconic stretch of road and so much a part of history to anyone who follows bike racing. Before long, the routine of getting into a fast group to make up time started again and we carried on towards Roubaix.

There were signs counting off each twenty kilometres that we had covered. At the last feed I filled myself up with a couple of cokes and a banana and a nice chap in a beret told me there were thirty kilometres left to cover. I never saw a sign for Roubaix in all this time, but noticed that the cobbled sectors had counted down to just one to go. I recognised the long straight run towards the velodrome from seeing it so many times on television. It's actually quite a steady climb, but I was so full of adrenaline that it didn't seem to matter. I saw one large building which looked like a stadium, but realised that it was too modern to be the velodrome. Then, over the rooftops I could see the floodlight pylons, again familiar from looking at photographs in magazines and books with Dicco.

There's one last piece of token cobbles on the approach to the velodrome, laid along the central reservation of a dual carriageway. It's very well maintained and relatively new, and seemed very artificial. Then a right turn, a long sweeping left, and the entry to the velodrome itself.

By some chance, I'd ridden the last few kilometres entirely on my own, which meant I got the chance to experience something else Dicco and I used to dream about. This really did feel just like I'd imagined. I was cruising along, head down, keeping up a reasonably (for me) good pace. Whenever I'd watched this race on television, it had given me memories of great riders, having distanced all their rivals, riding alone down this very bit of road, on the exact piece of tarmac that I was on. I rode into the stadium completely alone. I could hear the commentator on the PA, and enjoyed the brief applause of people lining the entrance, all probably eagerly awaiting someone they knew.

I must admit I was pretty overwhelmed thinking of some of the other riders whose wheel tracks I was now following. Not just the modern generations of greats like Tom Boonen and Fabian Cancellara but so many other names ran through my mind – Johan Museuw, Sean Kelly, Bernard Hinault, Roger de Vlaemick, Eddy Merckx, Fausto Coppi, and now, just for one fleeting moment in the mind of a forty something man another name could be added to that list... mine.

Another surge of adrenalin and emotion helped increase my speed as I came into the final straight. I'd lived this moment many times as a boy, so I knew exactly what to do. I came out of the last bend, pulled my jersey straight, adjusted my sunglasses to the right angle, sat up, lifted my arms in a glorious, if ironic, victory salute and coasted over the line.

A few seconds later I came across Richard and one of the tour organisers, jubilant that we'd finished. We soaked up the atmosphere then decided to go back to our hotel. In the excitement I forgot to have my photograph taken in the Eddy Merckx memorial shower cubicle or by the cobble stone sculpture. It only took a few minutes to find our hotel and drop off our bikes. I realised that my club mates would probably be somewhere on a club run so sent a text saying that I'd just ridden solo into the velodrome at Roubaix at the end of the ride. (I neglected to mention the several hundred people who'd done this ahead of me).

It took a while for me to calm down enough to phone home

but once I'd managed that it was time for a shower and a long drink of local beer. We waited at the hotel and saw other riders from our group arrive back. We watched the end of that day's real spring classic, the Tour of Flanders, on television before going out for a couple of beers in Roubaix. I'd certainly had times when I'd felt more exhausted after a ride but never had I felt so exhilarated. A group of us shared our stories of the day, and I couldn't fail to notice the tremor in both my hands as I picked up my glass. It had been more than worth the discomfort, and the following weekend I sat and watched Belgian rider Tom Boonen win the professional race. I couldn't help noticing that he took ten minutes longer than I did to complete the course. Not a bad result from my point of view, especially if you forget the fact that he'd ridden almost sixty miles further than me that day.

Maybe Dicco and I had got it wrong – maybe I should have forgotten my aspirations to be a climber in the Tour de France, spending hours climbing towards the clouds whilst making my appearance in cycling's equivalent of Hollywood and its technicolour wonders. Maybe I was a classics man, art house and black and white, getting my arms browned by the mud thrown up from the roads of Flanders, not the sunshine of the Alps and the Pyrenees.

Stage 14
Winter Woes

As summer draws to a close, the European racing season has its swansong – the Tour of Lombardy, romantically known as 'the race of the Falling Leaves'. I have always thought this conjures up a lovely picture of golden autumnal colours, pleasant temperatures and a chance to look back on the year. Riders will remember the harsh weather and conditions of the early season in Flanders, and then how they suffered in the heat of July. By the time the leaves start to fall, they will be glad that the weather is a little cooler, and be looking forward to some time at home and a chance to relax.

Having had my own taste of cobbles in the Paris Roubaix earlier in the year and having felt the stifling heat in July as I climbed the Alps in another Etape du Tour, I was now seeing the leaves start to fall from the trees and the weather get cooler. The difference being of course, that the cooler weather in Yorkshire isn't really very welcome.

The falling leaves I came across had a habit of becoming a wet and slippery road hazard, sometimes getting thrown up and caught in my wheels. When this happened to a club mate, Stuart Newton, he reached forward to rid himself of the irritation, only to misjudge his timing and put his hand into the spokes of his front wheel, catapulting himself over the handlebars in the process, resulting in a cracked vertebra in his neck. Once his fellow riders were sure he was OK, which was after the air ambulance had attended, and he'd been taken off to hospital, they showed solidarity and sympathy by sending him a get well card, stuffed with dried leaves.

It had got to the stage in the year when the number of those turning up for club runs in shorts were outnumbered by those keeping their legs warm with long tights. By late October the weather meant that all the summer bikes were safely away for the winter, ready to be polished and left until the following spring, once the salt had gone from the roads.

Winter bikes tend to be a law unto themselves. They are often put together from old parts that have become obsolete as their owner 'upgrades' to something better. This often leads to mismatched components of differing age that don't work quite as well as they should. Winter is also when, for the sake of everyone around you, mudguards should really be fitted to your bike.

The mudguards on my bike seemed to have two functions. Firstly, they stopped mud and grit and whatever other unpleasant things were covering the roads from being redistributed onto my clothes, into my eyes and all over my bike. Secondly, they moved around so much that no matter how many times I fiddled with them, at least one part of them would be rubbing a tyre and making a noise. Just as I would stop and sort out an annoying sound from my front mudguard, the rear one would decide that it wanted to move, meaning I had to stop again.

This was mainly due to the fact that the bike I was using in winter was another hand-me-down, and the frame wasn't designed to have mudguards fitted, so I had got some clip on ones, held onto my bike by what was little more than an elastic band. Stopping frequently when I was riding alone only inconvenienced me, so wasn't much of a problem but expecting club mates to keep stopping when we were out together must have been annoying and frustrating for them. At least I consoled myself with the fact that I wasn't the only person to suffer these problems. The silver lining to this particular cloud was that I saw it as an excuse to think about the time when I could buy another new bike.

There are some people who like winter, who look forward to cosy nights in, perhaps with a nice fire lit and a film to watch. I really don't like it as darkness descends earlier and earlier and there seems to be nothing but twilight, even in the middle of the day. To me it is a time when meeting for a club run means waiting in the cold, hearing the sounds of stamping feet and the clapping of gloved hands in an attempt to keep some warmth in your extremities. Most people present will spend the time waiting to set off lifting their bikes so that their wheels can be spun to locate the source of a new rubbing sound that was heard for the first time on the way from home that morning. Once we get going, scarves are pulled over faces, collars are turned up, and even during daylight hours, lights stay on. The sky stays leaden grey. On moorlands the horizon is so murky that land and sky blend into one. Despite layers of thermal clothing, all the hand slapping and toe curling inside your shoes, the cold gradually works into every part of your body, until it feels as if you can feel the shape of your bones. By the time we get home there is no talk of a nice pint in a sunny beer garden or a coffee on the terrace of a café. Everyone just wants to get home, clean as much of the mud off their bike as they can, and try and thaw themselves out.

On one occasion, a couple of members of the club had said that they wanted to spend their Sunday morning doing some time trial training. This would involve hard sessions along part of a local 'A' road that is used regularly in the summer by a few local clubs. Even though I had no intention of doing time trials, I thought it would make a change. It was club legend Malcolm who had come out on his time trial bike, and he was happy for me to follow in his wheel tracks as long as I could keep up and stay out of his way. There was a light rain falling as we set off and I was quite glad that I seemed to be able to keep up with him for the first few miles. As he repeated his runs, the temperature started to fall and the rain gradually got heavier. I could see the water running in a steady stream off the back of Malcolm's bike before bouncing up off the road and covering me in a thick layer of grime. I was getting soaked and as the temperature continued to fall, the now heavy rain turned to snow. It was so cold and miserable that even Malcolm admitted we should probably go home.

By the time I got back, I could barely move my hands or feet. I struggled to get the key into to lock of the door and then had to sit on the floor once I got inside, where all the snow gradually melted from me and into a huge pool of water on the hallway floor. It took about twenty minutes to get my gloves and shoes off before I went and ran a steaming hot bath to help me warm up. If there is such a thing as 'catching a chill', I certainly caught one that day. I spent the following week coughing and spluttering and could only speak with a croaky voice.

One way to avoid the worst of the winter weather was to become reacquainted with my turbo trainer, but I also started to join my Cappuccino club mates for some evening rides. We would meet regularly and wind our way out of town onto the moors, creating our own pool of light in the darkness of the countryside.

This gave me another lesson in how bike technology has improved since the days Dicco and I used to ride. During the winter months we would cycle to a primary school in the middle of Hull to take part in exercise sessions to ready ourselves for the next racing season. We would spend half our time stopping to try and get our 'Ever Ready' lights to work, usually taking them apart to bend the copper strips inside them to keep them in contact with a huge, often leaky, battery. As this never seemed to fix the problem for very long, we would usually resort to hitting them repeatedly every time they went out. The lights on display on any Cappuccino Club outing suffered no such problems. Modern lights are reliable and bright enough to dazzle motorists and in some cases, I'm sure, be seen from low flying planes, perhaps even from outer space.

Before joining the evening rides, I had been to a local shop to buy some lights that I had seen advertised on their website. It was around midday when I arrived and the man behind the counter was just chewing his way through a sandwich.

I saw the light I wanted on a display rack, apologised to him for disturbing his lunch as I handed my prospective purchase over to him and got ready to pay.

He looked at the price ticket and was so shocked that he coughed out half of his remaining sandwich in surprise.

'Twenty-seven bloody quid! 'He said. 'That's a bloody rip-off; it's not worth that much!'

It seemed a bit unusual to me for someone who was supposed to be selling me something to admit that he didn't think his goods were worth the money. I reassured him that I was happy with the price, as it was the same as any other shop where I'd seen the same light.

'No', he continued with what was now becoming something of a rant. 'It's bloody rubbish, you don't want it, the other ones are much better, this one's shite.'

He finished the rest of his sandwich and then opened the door into a cellar below the shop.

'Come and look at this', he said. I felt some trepidation at being invited into the cellar of a man whose behaviour was strange to say the least. He got some of the other lights off the same display stand where I had got mine from, and spent the next twenty minutes or so trying each of them out in turn by shining them into the darkness of the space below. I didn't feel able to leave as he was obviously trying to be helpful. We were briefly interrupted when the door opened and a boy of about ten came in.

The shop assistant looked him up and down and asked him what he wanted.

The boy had brought a BMX bike into the shop with him, and asked how much it would cost to have the brakes taken off it.

'I'm not taking the brakes off your bike son, now bugger off!'

The boy retreated and we were left to try out the rest of the lights. In the end I bought two lights instead of the one I had gone in for but actually spent less money than I would have done if I had been allowed to stick to my original choice.

Cycle lights, of course, aren't just designed to help you see where you're going, they help you to be seen by other road users, so as the winter wore on, they were a permanent fixture on my bike, apart from on the clearest, crispest of bright winter days.

Single speed, fixed wheel bikes have had a massive resurgence in recent years, having become something of a fashion statement on city streets all over Europe, and especially in London. They usually seem to be ridden by hipster types, with designer beards, slick clothes and messenger bags over their shoulders. These people seem to have a reputation not only for trying to look cool, but also for being a hazard to everyone else. If some social commentators are to be believed, they also represent any one of a long list of things that are wrong with modern Britain.

In my early teenage years as a member of the Hull Thursday Road Club many of the older club members would ride fixed wheel bikes throughout the winter months. The logic behind this idea was that as mileages were less in winter, the inability to free-wheel at any time meant that even though there wasn't time to ride as far, the miles ridden were doing you more good than if you could spend half the time free-wheeling.

Throughout the winter I often remembered club runs when many of the older members would ride their old fixed wheel bikes and began to wish I could get one to use. It seemed even more appropriate now that I was towards the older end of the age spectrum in the Cappuccino Cycling Club.

After asking around, I got hold of an old bike that was destined to be thrown away. I liked the fact that it was made by Carlton, the same company that had made the bikes Dicco and I used to ride. I stripped it down and reassembled it with a fixed wheel and had a lot of fun riding around town while seeing how long I could stay both upright and stationary at the same time. Being so old, and only having the most rudimentary brake, which I'd taken off an old child's bike before it got taken to the tip, it wasn't really suitable for a club run. Luckily, another opportunity for a free bike came about when a friend of mine needed some more room in his shed.

When we met up for him to give me the bike, I couldn't have been more delighted. It was made by an old frame builder from Bradford called Geoff Clark, whose name ran along its tubes. It had a suitable retro paint scheme – dark red with black panels and rainbow stripe detailing. It looked exactly like the type of bikes ridden by wizened old club men when Dicco and I were riding as teenagers.

I spent a happy day stripping it down and cleaning it up as much as I could. Even after a wash and polish, it still had a pleasing patina of age, which I decided to leave, instead of recreating the sort of mess I made last time I tried to repaint my bike all those years ago in mum and dad's garage. Some of the parts were seized up, so I had to take it to a bike shop to get them removed and new bits fitted, but after a day or two, I had the steel, fixed wheel bike I had been looking for. It seemed appropriate that it was of the same vintage as the ones I used to see on the winter club runs of my youth.

I was keen to use my new bike on a club run, and waited until I knew we were going to do a reasonably flat route and that there would be a few other people on similar bikes so that I wouldn't hold anyone up as a result of not having a range of gears to help me climb any hills.

It was Remembrance Sunday, and it was a clear and cold day, with little cloud and blue skies. We rode north from Harrogate, on nice flat roads, with scarce traffic. A couple of minutes before eleven o'clock, we rounded a gentle bend in the road and saw a small church up ahead. Its congregation was just coming outside to assemble at the small memorial by the roadside to observe two minutes silence. The road was narrow and as a group, we eased to a stop, unclipped ourselves from our pedals, and waited with them.

The sun was out and there was a clear view across the fields, which were ploughed ready to be sewn with seed. Unsure of exactly what to do next, we took off our helmets and watched the rest of the people file out of the church and gather in front of the stone pillar, engraved with the names of the young men who had left this little village a hundred years ago, and who never returned.

An older man stepped forward to recite the eulogy. Medals hung from his chest and I wondered what memories he must hold, which friend he was thinking of when he described how, 'age would not weary them'.

It was very poignant to have the honour to share those two minutes with people we had never met before. Afterwards, as they got ready to go back into church, they thanked us for taking the time to stop. There are no words to describe why no thanks were required but gratefully received nonetheless. We have been back there every year since, turning something that was spontaneous into what has become a club tradition in honour of the memories of the fallen.

November passed into December, with the prospect of Christmas and the new year, shorter club runs and more time on my turbo trainer. Since I have been cycling, the problem of what my family can get me for Christmas has been solved, so every year I get to add to my collection of books, socks, caps and water bottles and it is always a pleasure. I sometimes put these away as I wait for spring to come and make use of older ones that are already showing the wear and tear of being used throughout a Northern English winter.

Finally, just as I was about to get totally fed up of non-stop bike cleaning, cold wet feet and mudguards that were worse than useless, the weather began to warm up, the nights grew lighter, and cycling was back on the television. To me, these were the green shoots that meant spring was on its way. It also meant that I could finally get my summer bike out once again.

Most people around Harrogate look for the sea of flowers that begin to carpet the verges at the town's roadsides as a sign that winter is finally over and that spring has arrived. Summer sees the town's parks and gardens full of bright flower beds. As autumn comes, the roads out of town cross moors that are carpeted with purple heather, then the same moorlands are bleak and beautiful in equal measure though the winter months. This is how the year rolls around.

To me, the year has two much simpler seasons. I either ride my best bike or I ride my winter bike and best is always better than winter.

Stage 15
Perfect

A friend of mine was selling his house, he had arranged an open morning in an attempt to gain some interest from potential buyers. He had thrown the doors open to any interested parties to come and look around on a Sunday morning in spring. He asked if I would be there as a kind of 'rent a crowd', as he felt that if there were more people it would show the house in good light.

His home, a lovely old Victorian house, had large rooms and high ceilings. When I went in, sunlight was streaming through the windows, the radio was playing gently in the background, there were newspapers laid artfully on the sofa and a smell of fresh coffee. It was all designed to make the house look more homely and welcoming. Viewed like this, it seemed to me like the ideal setting for a perfect Sunday morning.

For most people, the ideal Sunday morning involves waking up late, having a leisurely breakfast while working their way through the Sunday papers. Later there might be a little walk to the pub and a big meal, probably allowing time for a contented nap at some point during the afternoon.

At about the time I went to help make my friend's house look more saleable this would have been pretty close to my favourite way of spending a day when I had nothing to worry about, other than what time to put the vegetables on to go with the roast. Now though, I had reached the stage where a day like this would have been something of a nightmare.

If I wasn't able to go out on my bike on Sunday morning, even if this was because we were busy doing something else, I would gradually feel more and more restless, unable to truly settle to anything. Being stuck at home was the worst; I would find myself pacing about, looking out at the weather and thinking how nice it would be to be out on my bike. My idea of a relaxing Sunday didn't involve anything that would normally be viewed as taking things easy in the same way as most people.

In his book 'The Rider' Tim Krabbe describes how he arrives in a village in central France to take part in a race through the local mountains. As he is getting ready, he looks around, he sees people relaxing in the street cafés near the start. He says he is shocked by the emptiness that non-racers must feel in their lives. I didn't think of non-cyclists as having particularly empty lives but had got to the point where I wondered what I used to do on Sunday mornings when I couldn't get up to go on a club run.

I had reached the stage where my ideal Sunday would start early, with the sun streaming between the gaps in the curtains. I would creep downstairs and get a decent breakfast ready – a big bowl of porridge with raisins and maple syrup, even in summer, because of its high carbohydrate content. I'd finish this off with poached eggs on toast, fruit and a nice cup of tea.

Once I had my kit on, the last thing I would do before leaving the house would be to drain a double espresso. I had read somewhere that this was a good thing to do and as I have always liked espresso it was nice to drink it without feeling guilty about the fact that current opinion seems to say that it is not very good for you to drink too much coffee.

With this in mind, I was glad to wake up to a beautiful summer's morning. It had been a warm night and I crept downstairs as quietly as I could. The air was so warm that I opened the kitchen door whilst I got my breakfast ready and enjoyed the holiday-like feeling this gave me as I sat and ate, overlooking the garden.

An hour or so later, after enjoying my by now traditional double espresso, I wheeled my bike down to the garden gate, clipped my feet to the pedals and set off to meet my club mates. The temperature was such that I was in short sleeves and the forecast was so good that I hadn't needed to stuff a rain jacket into my pockets. I just had my usual emergency kit – the things needed to change a punctured tube, a chain tool and an Allen key. These were supplemented by the ultimate get-out-of jail card; a wallet containing a mobile phone, a credit card and a few pounds to spend in the café later.

It was pleasant winding my way towards our meeting place. Most of the people I saw seemed to be up because they wanted to be, not because they had to rush to work and nearly everyone I saw nodded or spoke some form of greeting. By the time I got to the gates of the school where we meet, there were already a few others there, chatting away happily and waiting in the sunshine. No need to adjust loose mudguards or clear leaves from wheels and spokes, just a fleet of best bikes, and shiny kit, ready for a good day out.

Although the attitude of motorists and other road users was much better since Bradley Wiggins won the Tour de France, (it was now at least three weeks since someone had last sworn at us), there were far too many of us to ride as one group, so we spent a few minutes sorting ourselves out. This meant that there was one steady group, two medium groups and a fast one, which I joined. By this time I had realised that the main goal of my 'training', if I had to call it that, was to be able to ride with the faster group each Sunday, feel that I could contribute to the workload without slowing everyone down and to the conversation without being too breathless to speak.

After a few minutes we set off. We rode through town, enjoying the fact that the temperature was rising nicely and looking forward to leaving suburbia behind as we headed north into the Dales. As the town's roads gave way to countryside, the group settled into its own rhythm. Heading north out of Harrogate meant that we were steadily climbing for the first few miles. The gradient never got too steep and it was nice to see the surrounding moors slowly coming into view. As I looked around, I realised that, at some point in the last few years, I had cycled over the horizon in every direction, from the Vale of York behind us, the Howardian

Hills distantly to our right and the Yorkshire Dales in front of us.

We crested the brow of the first hill and could see up the valley ahead, a mixture of woods, fields and deep blue reservoirs, our route took us left down a short hill and across one of them, its surface mirror-like in the peace of the early morning.

The air around the reservoir was cooler. As we climbed through the trees it was cooler still before we started climbing again, up a narrow gravel strewn road. For the first time, the group began to spread out, but we were soon back together, gathering our breath as the terrain levelled once more.

Despite the fact that we had spent much of the last half an hour or so ascending, there were still more hills before our route would take us over into Wharfedale. The road snaked out before us, dipping out of sight before climbing steeply onto a heather covered moor. I felt and heard the rush of the wind as we dropped downhill, before a brutally steep, but mercifully short climb. I tried to carry as much speed as I could, but as the uphill gradient and rough road took away my momentum, I began to click, one by one, into lower gears to help me to the top. We crested the moor to be greeted with a view that reached up Wharfedale. To our left, and below us, was another glistening mass of water. Above it the telephone mast on the top of Norwood Edge, a hill I have climbed more times than I can count. Over our right shoulders the horizon was much more distant, being formed by hills that lay over thirty miles away, with the White Horse of Kilburn just visible through the haze. Those climbs would be left for another day.

This was the first flat piece of road we had ridden along since leaving Harrogate, and it was a good chance for everyone to have a quick drink and maybe even a bite of an energy bar. We got the first reward for all our climbing as we turned down a long descent. In one line on the traffic free road, we crouched as low as we could and let gravity take us down the hill.

There was more downhill to come even after we had to stop at the bottom of the first hill, before the road bobbed up and down until we began to follow the river and the road was flat again for a while. We had the river to our left, to our right the hill that we would soon turn up.

The climb back up to the moors was the sort of satisfying ride that made me feel fitter and faster than I really am. Sometimes these type of climbs are called 'tempo climbs', because although it takes effort to get up them, you never feel yourself suffering too much. Because the gradient is constant, the effort is easier to manage.

The road dipped in and out of woods, giving us some shade until we emerged onto open moorland, crossing a cattle grid as we did so. Our route seemed to be hugging the hillside, running parallel to the top of the hill, as if it wanted to give us some chance of rest. We passed a couple of small farms, still riding closely together and enjoying each other's company, chatting when the effort wasn't too much to make talking difficult.

We were approaching the last part of the climb now. Once again the road dipped and gave us some rest before finally turning toward the top of the hill, this time seeming to want to remind us that climbing is never meant to be easy. Round the last bend we all had to stand to keep momentum. With one last effort and one last turn to the left we crested the hill. The group had broken up by now, so we soft pedalled until we were all together again.

We were well rewarded for our efforts; there was a fantastic view to admire before a long, open descent with no sharp bends and open views of the road ahead. Once we had regrouped, the real sounds of a club run filled our ears. The clicking of gears, bits of conversation as we chatted and the occasional whirring as we free-wheeled when the road allowed us to. There were the sounds of the surrounding countryside too – the rustle of leaves in the trees and the call of curlews as the swooped around above us.

As much as getting me fit for all the events I had done, I realised that it was on days like this that all the time I had spent twiddling away on my turbo trainer had been worthwhile. In a way, cycling is about suffering, especially when you have set yourself a challenge that you know will push you to the very limits of your abilities. It is very satisfying to ride up a famous foreign mountain and part of that satisfaction comes from the fact that the experience will make you reach into yourself to find that extra bit of will power to overcome pain and exhaustion. At the time it can be brutally unpleasant, but the memory of such days on the bike is almost always a positive one. Today though, wasn't about pushing myself or suffering, I just wanted to enjoy the benefits of feeling fit, and being able to spend my day with friends, enjoying the simple pleasure of the bicycle.

We had been going for a couple of hours by now and our attention began to focus on our café stop, just a few miles further ahead. The road rolled along the side of the valley. Through the gaps in the trees we could see green fields and cattle, with the occasional glimpse of the river which, eventually, in the distance we could see meandering towards a village. We knew it wouldn't be long before we would be sitting relaxing in the sunshine.

The café was already busy with a mixture of hikers, holiday makers and other cyclists. We sat at a table outside, taking in the warmth of the sun. The village green was in front of us and to the left was the old pub and a bridge over the gently flowing river. We could see back up the road we had just ridden on our way here, with the fell rising sharply above the line of trees where the green fields gave way to heather. It looked stunning in the late summer sunshine and we chatted happily as we refuelled ourselves with beans on toast, tea and cakes. As we chatted someone noticed our Cappuccino Cycling Club jerseys, and asked us how come we were a club who owned our own bus. Even three years later, the day when we borrowed a bus still draws comments from people who saw it and we usually find ourselves saying it is currently in for a service so hasn't been seen for a while.

It was so pleasant sitting outside that café that we really didn't want to leave but the arrival of more and more cyclists prompted us to get moving again. We didn't really have any choice other than to take a hilly route home, so we set off steadily.

Despite the even pace, I still suffered 'café legs'. It always seems to take a couple of miles for me to find my rhythm after stopping, and this morning was no exception. After a few minutes I began to feel that the positive effects of our break where overcoming the stiffness I felt in my legs as we got going again.

The road criss-crossed the river, taking us in and out of the shade of the trees, through villages made up of stone cottages and small farm houses. People were just beginning to gather at tables outside the front of pubs, ready for an early Sunday pint and probably a large lunch.

We were heading for the steepest climb of the day, and as we turned onto the road leading to the point where it suddenly reared up, we rode closely together, knowing that our differing pace up the hills would mean that we would soon be spread out but also silently agreeing that we would re-group once we reached the top.

Even when riding in a group, a really steep hill soon makes me drift into a world of my own, and as I looked upwards, towards the next bend where the road switched back on itself I had to concentrate on my own speed, trying to balance my effort with the need to conserve energy for later in the climb. I reached a state where I was only vaguely aware of the whereabouts of the rest of the group, some of whom were behind me, others so close that I could hear their breathing as they entered their own battle with the gradient. Before long, as the road levelled off a little, I found I could sit down again and pedal more smoothly. For the next couple of miles, I had the feeling that I was more evenly matched with the hill than its lower slopes had allowed me to be, and started to enjoy the rewarding feeling of seeing the top of the hill get closer and closer.

Even though the day was supposed to be just about a steady ride, there was a definite feeling of satisfaction at having at least suffered for a little while, as if a rush of endorphins just increased the overall enjoyment of the day. We rested at the top of the climb until everyone had regained their breath and looked in the direction of the route home. In the same way as children on long car journeys always seem to be asking, 'Are we there yet?' we still hadn't finished climbing for the day. As time had gone on, a fairly strong wind had developed and we had to ride head long into it up the last steep hill. Even though the top looked to be only a short way off, the road dragged steadily uphill for at least another mile, before we reached its true summit, marked with a sign welcoming us back into Nidderdale. This really was the point where the really hard effort was over and it was nice to see the right turn back towards Harrogate and home.

Knowing that the end of a ride is close always gives an extra bit of energy and the group's speed steadily increased on the long, shallow descent towards the end of our journey. The road was wide and straight and it was a pleasure to ride as a tightly knit group, keeping a good pace for the last few miles. At last, we rode into town, as people began to relax and think about what to do with the rest of their day.

I sometimes like to go for a post ride coffee, but today the weather was so good and the frothy pints of beer that I had seen people enjoying outside the pubs we had passed made me suggest a quick post ride pint instead. Everyone agreed this would be a nice way to finish off and we made our way to one of the town's pubs with a sunny beer garden.

The inside of the pub was almost silent as we entered, with just a few drinkers standing at the bar. A couple of them were engaged in conversation but most were just quietly enjoying a solitary lunchtime pint. After disrupting the peaceful atmosphere as we fumbled in jersey pockets to find money and sort out bits of discarded food, we took our drinks out into the garden, moved a couple of tables together, and sat down. I took a long gulp on my pint and sat back happily.

The setting was almost perfect – neat flower beds surrounded a well-kept lawn, and the sun was high in a cloudless sky. For the second time that day I found myself simply enjoying the company of my club mates, talking happily and feeling very relaxed and contented. We sat for a while, reflecting on a great day out on our bikes. We remembered the sights and sounds of the places we had passed through, and the tough bits of the route. Those in the group who had computers had left them on their bikes – number crunching and recording of distances and height climbed could come later, interesting though it would be. We simply sat, talked, laughed, and felt very lucky that we were able to take pleasure from the bicycle, one of the greatest inventions known to mankind, that we were lucky enough to do so in some of the most beautiful scenery imaginable.

I could have happily sat there until the sun went down, but I needed to be home, to hang my bike up, ready for another perfect day.

Stage 16
Yellow Fever

One Sunday in August 2012, the members of the Cappuccino Cycling Club were in a small yard, outside a coffee shop hidden amongst the alleyways of York. It was a glorious English summer's day and there was the usual high turn-out, with about forty riders who had assembled for the ride in the early morning sunshine. Nice and flat, not too far, and a café stop to look forward to.

It was only a couple of weeks since Bradley Wiggins had taken the gold medal in the Olympic time trial in London, which followed on from his historic Tour de France win, where another British rider, Chris Froome, had come second. The British track team had done well in the Olympic Velodrome with local girl Lizzie Armistead taking silver medal in the women's road race. Elite British cycling truly was in the best place it had ever been. Even at our level things were different. Earlier that day, a group of teenage boys had seen us ride past, one of them had shouted 'Is Wiggo with you?' which was much nicer than the usual abuse that we had grown used to. Cyclists, it seemed, whilst not exactly becoming popular, were at least hated a bit less by other road users.

I finished my post-ride snack of eggy bread, maple syrup and bacon and drained my cup of tea. I was feeling very content and felt like sharing my feelings. 'You know what?' I asked no one in particular, 'There will never be a better time to be a cyclist in this country'. Bearing in mind what had happened that year, it was a reasonable assumption, but none of us sitting in the sunshine on that Sunday could have possibly imagined how wrong I was.

A few months later I was away at a training meeting with my work colleagues. Having helped set the whole thing up, I was tasked with making the opening remarks in which I encouraged everyone present to make the most of the day and concentrate as much as they could.

Just as I had finished my presentation and sat down, I noticed that my phone was flashing to tell me I had a text. I get very frustrated when I see people looking at their phones in meetings, so I ignored it.

It wasn't long before a break in proceedings meant I could see what the message had to say. By this time, there were several messages waiting for me, from all sorts of family and friends. The first one said 'Tour de France starting in Yorkshire'. The next said 'Stage one of the tour is going to finish in Harrogate'. There were numerous others and by piecing them together I realised that the 2014 Tour de France was going to be in my home county for two days. Not only that, but the first stage was going to finish in my home town and on the second day, the route would pass directly in front of my house.

There are not enough clichés to describe how I felt. So I avoided checking the date, pinching myself or re-reading the label of the bottle of water in the middle of the table to check it wasn't full of vodka. There had been strong rumours in the weeks before the announcement but I don't think anyone really thought they would come true. It was already well know that there was a good chance that the Tour would be starting somewhere in the United Kingdom, but the smart money was on the British Cycling backed plan of Edinburgh hosting the start. We all knew that Yorkshire had put in a bid and had of course been hopeful but I don't think anyone really believed that it would be chosen over the other offers that were on the table.

This truly was something that I could never have imagined would happen. I remember as a child spending many happy holidays in France. We always went by car and I kept myself occupied, for the many hours when I wasn't fighting with my brother in the back seat, looking out for signs that we were on a road that had been used in the Tour de France. I'd mostly look for the graffiti that the fans paint across the tarmac, as these would be the most obvious. Failing that, I'd try to recognise the names of towns that I might have read about and look at distant mountains wondering if the roads I could see climbing up their sides were any of the legendary ascents from the Tour. I can remember the time I gazed for ages at Mont Ventoux, visible in the far distance as we drove South on the motorway. At that time, even driving along a road that had once been part of the Tour de France would have filled me with excitement. The news I had just heard meant that I wouldn't need to dream about those roads any more – I could actually see one without even having to get out of bed.

I spent the rest of the day in a daze, and certainly didn't get as much out of the training course as I should have. The Tour de France was the only thing I could talk about to anyone at lunchtime and the first thing I mentioned when I phoned to say that I was on my way home.

By the time of the next club run, the conversation was about little else. Everyone was incredibly excited and wondering just how it would all work out. The full route of the two Yorkshire stages had already been published so we were even able to start talking about where we would all choose to go and watch. In one moment of eager over optimism, I even had a look to see how much it would cost to rent a helicopter for the day so I could go and see some of the climbs in the Dales and still be back in time to see the finish in Harrogate. It wasn't as expensive as I thought, but I settled on a plan of a short ride to see the peloton pass by in the early part of the stage, before cycling back to Harrogate in time for the finish.

Naturally, anyone I spoke to who knew I was a keen cyclist would ask me if I was excited about the Tour coming to town. It seemed impossible to explain to them just how momentous an event this was. 'Can you imagine', I would say 'If they cancelled Wimbledon and moved it to Harrogate tennis club?'

'But that would never happen.'

'Exactly.'

'Or if FIFA turned up at Harrogate Town's ground and said they wanted to have the world cup final there?'

'Now you're being ridiculous.'

'I know – it will be even bigger than that.'

In truth, it was impossible to exaggerate the scale of it all. The Tour is the biggest annual sporting event in the world with many millions of people watching those opening two days on television. It would bring massive publicity on a global scale to a small town in Yorkshire and millions of pounds into the wider local economy. It was equally impossible to explain the amount of boyish excitement it was all causing for thousands of middle aged cyclists who could usually be seen around the county's roads every Sunday.

The impending arrival of the world's biggest cycling event gradually started to make people other than keen cyclists get excited. The local media carried endless stories of what to expect, and how it was all going to work. I kept being tempted into buying extra newspapers simply because their billboards said things like 'Latest info – where to see the Tour'. These inevitably turned out to be a disappointment, usually only telling me something I already knew or carrying a special feature of someone who had knitted a novelty yellow jersey for their dog or built a bike shaped hamster cage.

The event seemed to capture the imagination of the public. Car accessory shops must have been amazed at the amount of yellow spray paint they sold as everywhere around Yorkshire yellow bikes began to appear. They would hang from railings, adorn traffic islands and dangle from lamp posts. Although a lot of them were obviously old children's bikes, I couldn't help wondering that some of the bikes that had been dug out from sheds and garages could have been quite rare and exotic and had been used for decoration without anyone realising their value or potential. A bit like when an edition of 'Antiques Roadshow' turns up a Ming vase that has been used as a doorstop for the last fifty years. There must have been more than one person who was finally inspired to get his old bike back from his parents house so he could start cycling again, only to find that it had been sprayed yellow and hung from a tree.

Across the county, farmers dyed their sheep yellow. Houses were painted with the colours of the leader's jerseys. Bunting began to appear everywhere. One of the pubs in Harrogate even changed its name from The Coach and Horses to 'The "Cvndsh" and Horses' complete with a new sign with a picture of Mark Cavendish. Most of the other pubs sold at least one commemorative real ale. It would have been rude of me not to try at least a few pints of each and our club web site was full of images of beer pumps with pictures of bikes or cycling on them, because nearly every other member had the same idea.

I spent a very happy afternoon with my youngest son preparing our own contribution to the yellow bike plague by spraying an old bike of his yellow and hanging it from the front of my house. My mum made a long line of yellow bunting and we complemented this with a big Yorkshire flag and some little French ones. I was quite pleased with the overall effect, having ignored the usual piece of decorating advice that 'less is more'. Even houses that were a good distance away from the route were decorated. Yellow and green and patches of red spots appeared almost everywhere.

As the date grew closer the excitement increased. One of my club mates was driving back into Harrogate when he saw Mark Cavendish, in full team kit, sitting with his bike at the point where the finish line was going to be. He did a speedy U-turn, took a photo and had it on the club web site in minutes, thus giving himself a head start in the 'pro-cyclist stalker' competition. Every so often a whole team would be seen, making reconnaissance rides along the route. This culminated when Team Sky were spotted at a large hotel just outside town. A few members of the Cappuccino Cycling Club rode there and had a happy hour pestering the mechanics and having their photos taken with some of the riders. The morning finished as they followed some of the team, complete with support cars and police outriders as they set off on a training ride. I only wished I hadn't decided to do some jobs around the house that morning so that I could go on the club run the next day with a clear conscience.

All kinds of wild rumours began to circulate. If these were to be believed then apparently there were going to be nearly three million people in Harrogate on the day of the tour. As Harrogate has a population of about seventy thousand, the sort of chaos that so many visitors could cause could only be imagined. Every single road was going to be closed and staff in the local shops were all going to have to sleep on the shop floor because they weren't going to be able to get to work. Mobile phones weren't going to work (this one actually came true), and someone had paid Betty's Tea Rooms over a hundred thousand pounds for use of their upstairs windows, which had a view of the finishing straight. All these stories, and many more were fuelled by an ever increasing level of excitement.

As May rolled into June Harrogate started to get ready. Signs began to appear warning of parking restrictions, and planning notices went up on lamp posts. These carried footnote 'Tdf operations' to explain why they were there. Along what was to be the finishing straight all of the flower beds were emptied as if it was autumn, sacrificing a large part of the Victorian splendour for which the town is so famous. The traffic islands over the last two or three miles of the course were all taken out and replaced with plastic temporary ones. With every little change the sense of anticipation grew.

One benefit to the local community that was much needed was the resurfacing of the local roads. This was to be expected – the climate in Yorkshire means pot holes are an ever present menace, and these had to be filled in before the arrival of the peloton. The irony was that much of the tour route would be run over main roads, which are rarely used by cyclists. It would be motorists that would feel the most discernible difference after the race had moved on.

As the countdown went from months to weeks, then to days, the Tour arrived properly. A huge area of the Stray, Harrogate's famous area of town centre common land, was laid with mesh to protect the grass, and a temporary arena was built to house a fan park, complete with food stalls, souvenir stands, a huge television screen and a stage.

I had to drive back from the South of England one day and as I passed Nottingham the signs above the motorway carried warnings about the disruption the Tour was expected to cause. I even saw a few team cars on their way to Yorkshire. I had the slightly surreal experience of seeing a member of staff from one of the teams in my local supermarket buying bottles of mineral water. If Id bumped into someone like him in a French supermarket on a childhood family holiday, I would have been pestering him for an autograph, regardless of the fact that he was part of the team's back room staff and not a famous rider.

Every single one of these things made me feel as excited as I had all those years ago in the back of our family car when I thought I'd seen somewhere famous from the Tour. In the final week, almost overnight, the entire infrastructure of the race was set up in the town centre, with hospitality caravans and grandstands being put in place.

We had enjoyed glorious weather for many weeks through May and June but as I took a stroll around the finish area just two days before the race was going to arrive, I couldn't believe that I could feel rain falling. The entrance to the fan park was starting to get muddy even with the modest number of people who were coming and going.

I knew that the organisers would have done a fantastic job and given the right weather the whole thing was going to look fantastic as it was beamed out to a global audience. I also knew that poor weather could potentially ruin everything. I could only hope that things would brighten up by the morning.

As I live in the town where the first stage was to finish, it would have felt unfair if I hadn't invited a few people to stay. Pretty soon after the tour's visit had been announced I had promised anyone who had asked about accommodation in Harrogate a place to stay at my house, even to the extent of offering my modest lawn as a free camp site. By the time the weekend came around, my Dad and brother had one room, cycling fan and friend from work Lesley and her husband Ian had come down from Scotland (having forgiven Yorkshire for 'stealing' their chance to host the Tour), to take another. The last space went to another friend, Gareth. He was originally going to come on his own, but had phoned me earlier in the week to ask if there was also room for his seven year old son Thomas, who had appeared at his bedside in the middle of the previous night to plead with his dad to be allowed to come and see the Tour de France.

Everyone started to arrive on the Friday evening. My girlfriend Lesley and I walked up to Harrogate railway station and waited in the real ale pub by the platform. It was full of visitors, most of whom were obviously cycling fans, many sampling yet more of the special commemorative beers that were on offer. Once Lesley and Ian had arrived from Scotland, we took a walk across town and round the fan park to gain a taste of the atmosphere. Everyone else arrived during the course of the evening, and after a couple of welcome drinks we tried our best to get an early night. It felt just like Christmas Eve as a child - going to bed full of excitement, and willing sleep to come so that the morning would come round sooner.

Finally, I opened my eyes and realised that today I was going to see the Tour de France. Not only that, I was going to see it twice and have a whole day to soak up the atmosphere, to be part of a day that would surely go down as one of the most memorable in the whole history of Harrogate. It was a day that no one truly thought would happen, but here it was.

On this day, all over the planet, people would be sitting down to watch the first day of the Tour de France on television and if they looked carefully, they might just spot a middle aged man in the crowd, wearing a Cappuccino Cycling Club t-shirt, standing, stunned in disbelief, as he experienced something he had dreamed about since he had first seen those television pictures all those years ago and his Grandad had promised him a new bike for Christmas.

Stage 17
Marking the Occasion

One of the more pleasant aspects of being in a cycling club is the social life it can provide. The Cappuccino Cycling club have a monthly night in a local pub, so that we can meet up to discuss anything club related and give our respective other halves a night off from hearing us talk about bikes.

Much as we do our best on these occasions to try and vary the topics of conversation, bikes and cycling tend to be the mainstay of what we talk about. On one of the nights in the pub, we had got onto the subject of 'Strava'. For the uninitiated, this is an internet based forum where anyone can download records of their rides, either from a bike computer or mobile phone, and compare them to other people who have ridden the same stretch of road. It can also be a way of recommending new ideas for routes or club runs. It can be a useful training tool and helpful if you want to compare your own rides over the same route to see if your fitness regime is working. On the flip side, it also allows those who wish to do so, to have the sort of conversations that would make a discussion about drying paint feel exciting.

Once the fact that the Tour de France was going to start in Yorkshire had been announced, we often spent our monthly 'first Friday beers' talking about our plans for the big weekend. Where and how we were going to enjoy the whole event. It was fairly late on one of these sociable evenings when someone came up with the idea of members of the club recording their own Strava time for the finishing straight of the stage into Harrogate, so that later we could compare it to the professionals.

This may sound like quite an interesting thing to do, but unfortunately the road that was to be used is very busy, has traffic lights on it, is full of wandering tourists trying to get a table in Betty's tea rooms and worst of all, it is part of the town's one way system. At the end of the first stage, the riders would be riding in the opposite direction to the way the traffic would normally travel. Not a problem to them obviously, as the road would be closed but a big problem to anyone trying to emulate them before the big day. A few more pints allowed imaginations to run wild enough to find a solution to this – we'd simply wait until about four o'clock one morning and try our luck when the roads were quiet. A few of us would keep look out whilst we took it in turns to time ourselves over the last few hundred metres of the stage. As we'd be the first and only people to do this, our record would stand until it was broken by someone like Mark Cavendish as he took victory in stage one before taking the first yellow jersey of the tour, which, at that time, was still something we were all sure would happen.

Thankfully, good sense meant that no one ever tried this, but there was still a desire to do something very special to mark the occasion of the Tour coming to our home town. Another night in the pub and the seeds of a much better idea were sewn. It was Jonathan Cave who first came up with the notion of riding from the start of the Tour in Yorkshire to the finish in Paris. His idea was that we could ride up to Harewood House, the stately home on the outskirts of Leeds that would mark the official start line, then make our way to Hull. We'd then sail overnight to Zebrugge in Belgium and spend the next couple of days getting all the way to Paris before riding around the Arc de Triomphe and along the Champs Elysees to cross the finish line of the Tour. The plan meant that we would arrive in Paris on the Saturday of the final weekend of the Tour so that we could see the professionals complete the last stage, hopefully with another win for Mark Cavendish on the day and a successful title defence by Chris Froome.

This turned out to be one of those beer fuelled ideas that

actually seemed more possible and credible in the cold light of day. Jonathan admirably took it upon himself to head up the organisation. He very kindly volunteered his wife Sarah to help him and persuaded a couple of other members of the club to add support. It wasn't long before he was drumming up participants, then taking deposits. He spent hour upon hour poring over maps to come up with a suitable route, which he then checked time and again by looking at the roads over the internet to make sure they were suitable to ride on – you can't always tell from a map whether a road is a dirt track or a dual carriageway so he wanted to be sure. By the time July arrived, everything was in place and we had even commissioned a commemorative club jersey for us all to wear as we rode into Paris. Jonathan called it 'the ride of a lifetime' – which it certainly promised to be. We weren't even going to be burdened with having to carry anything on our bikes, because he had arranged for support vans to follow us on our way.

There were two options for the ride, taking three or four days, depending on how far anyone wanted to go or felt they could, ride. The start point was to be Prologue Performance Cycling in Harrogate, from where we would ride up to the start line of the race proper at Harewood House and then set off for Paris.

Places like Prologue have sprung up as part of the recent cycling boom. They are totally different from the bike shops of my youth. In those days, places like Cliff Pratt's in Hull catered for the whole of the bicycle market. This meant that they would be cluttered with bikes of all sizes, from small children's bikes, shopping and commuter bikes and just about everything else. There would be a small section for what Dicco and I would consider 'proper' bikes and equipment, where exotic bits and pieces would be on sale, often underneath a poster of one of the continental stars of the day. People who worked in these places had to multi-task, fixing as well as selling bikes and would have to wipe greasy hands on their aprons when they needed to serve a customer. The walls behind the counter would have hundreds of little drawers and cardboard boxes stacked up, carrying labels saying things like 'size 2 cotter pins' or 'three eights number four'. The fact that everywhere was piled so high with clutter meant that the interiors were dark and dingy. Modern shops are totally different – they are light and airy, almost exclusively showing off expensive and desirable bikes, wheels and clothing. Instead of the smell of grease and woodbines, it is the scent of espresso and cake that fills the air. Going into a bike shop now is a much nicer experience than it ever used to be.

Prologue's owner, John Reid, had agreed to sponsor the ride and provided everyone with a water bottle and a generous supply of energy gels and bars. The first group would set off for Paris on the Wednesday, and the rest of us would leave the next day, giving us three days to get to Paris.

The weekend when the Tour de France itself came to Harrogate was going to be hugely exciting and now there really was a way to mark to occasion. Making use of the multitude of skills at our disposal, we had some pocket sized route books printed by one member of the club, Mark Summersall, with road captain Martin Procter using his artistic talent to design the covers, which carried the lines:

'The ride of a lifetime, celebrating the start and finish of the Tour de France, in the beautiful surroundings of the great outdoors.

Inspired by bird song, and the colours and fragrances of the countryside. In the company of committed and like-minded companions,.

Riding the most remarkable and inspiring machine ever devised.... *the bicycle'*

In the weeks leading up to the ride, most of us realised that it gave us an excuse to buy some new bits of kit. Like most people with an all-consuming hobby, I resent spending money on clearly uninteresting but vital things like household maintenance and furniture but can nearly always find an excuse to buy something cycling related. There was no reason to think that a ride from Yorkshire, across Belgium and into France towards Paris rendered anything anyone owned obsolete but there was a noticeable increase in the number of new pairs of shoes and sunglasses on display when we met for our regular club runs. Every one of the participants was delighted with the special jerseys, which had a clever Eiffel tower design on one sleeve, and even the initials 'HD' printed on one of the pockets, as seen on the jerseys real riders wear for their three week, rather than three day, marathon.

I wondered how best to get ready for a ride like this. I don't often get the chance to ride on consecutive days, and when I do it certainly never involves day after day of long rides. Club runs are traditionally held on Sundays, so everyone goes back to work on Monday, instead of going on another long ride. Family and other commitments meant that adding another ride on Saturdays wouldn't really be an option either. We just did as many long days in the saddle as we could. On the day after these I would try to do a hard session on my turbo trainer instead of resting like I usually did.

One day in early spring, someone suggested the idea of doing a 'fixed wheel century' – riding a hundred miles on our single speed, fixed wheel bikes. This would be good preparation for our ride to Paris. I needed to do as many long rides as I could in the months leading up to July, and doing such a long ride without the option of free-wheeling would be a good test of stamina.

Six of us enjoyed a fantastic day out, even though one member of the group, Dave, turned up on a bike with gears. We agreed he could come with us as long as he promised not to use them. It was probably a hard thing to do – to go against the instinctive desire to change gear in relation to the terrain. Aside from the low tech bikes we were riding, we didn't have any of the GPS units that we would be using on our trip to France and had also managed to come out without any maps. We started on familiar roads, before heading north out of York and spending a couple of hours on roads that seemed to go vaguely in the direction we wanted them to. It was a nice feeling to simply go where the roads took us and we eventually started to see signs for the town of Thirsk, where we parked our bikes outside York's Tea Room. There was one of the thousands of yellow bikes that had appeared all over Yorkshire in the window. The walls were adorned with cycling jerseys and pictures so we felt very welcome as we sat down to refuel on tea and cakes.

The owner was pleased to have some cyclists in his café, and took photos of us and our bikes to post on his Facebook page. It was nice to feel that cyclists are now seen as people who should be made welcome, rather than being viewed as nothing more than a sweaty inconvenience as had so often been the case in the past.

By the time we got home, a hundred miles on a fixed wheel bike certainly felt like an achievement in itself, and it was nice to feel that it would help my fitness as I got ready to set off to Paris.

I set myself the target of doing at least one hundred mile ride every month as a way of getting my body used to longer distance riding. There were countless long rides to take part in being organised via the Cappuccino club website and everyone was doing as much as they could to be ready. I rode a few events, including the route of stage one of the Tour around the roads of Yorkshire. As I rode over the line I heard my name being called out and I found Lesley waiting for me, with a cool bottle of Daleside Blonde which was the most enjoyable way possible of rehydrating after the day's ride.

With only a week or so to go before we set off for Paris, I started to feel that at last I was ready. Until, that is, when someone came up with the idea that it would be *de rigueur* to complement all our special matching kit with matching, hairless legs.

I was no stranger to this – Dicco and I had shaved our legs all those years ago, even before we had enough hair on our chins to justify owning a razor. The idea of smooth legs for our ride to Paris possibly came about at one of the club 'meetings' in the Swan on the Stray, probably quite late on when imaginations had been fuelled by a few pints. It was just the sort of idea that gathers momentum and takes hold of a group of people. Once one person had agreed to do it, no one really had the option to say no.

We live in a society where, rightly or wrongly, women shave their legs, so I decided that I'd seek the advice of my girlfriend, Lesley, as to the best way to achieve a smooth, aerodynamic surface to my well trained legs. Taking one look at the thick hair that had grown since the days when I shaved my legs as a teenager, she advised that either waxing or chemicals were my only options, because the thickness of the hair that needed removing meant using a razor would quite likely result in a messy blood bath. I had seen enough video clips of men undergoing waxing, either through drunkenness or for charity, to put me off suffering that ordeal, so I chose chemical removal. She agreed to help me so, one trip to the pound shop later, I was ready with two bottles of something called 'Nair'.

One evening, in the days just before I was due to set off to Paris and after a pleasant meal and a couple of glasses of wine, we decided it was time to complete my preparations. I stood, trouser-less, in my bath whilst Lesley used a kind of spatula to spread the strange smelling substance all over my legs. She is something of a perfectionist and although I was happy to stop the process at about the place my cycling shorts reach, she took over, pointing out that any job worth doing, is worth doing right. I was beginning to get a little worried by the strange sensation all over my skin, and was trying to elicit a bit of sympathy, only to be told to stop complaining and that women across the world have to undergo this regularly. She asked me to turn around to give better access to some area on the back of my thigh, before saying something along the lines of, 'This is not good'.

Feeling vulnerable, I was a bit worried by this and asked what the problem was. She told me she couldn't reach certain parts of my legs and told me to get out of the bath and stand on the lid of the closed toilet.

I had visions of one of my children suddenly realising that they had left something vital in the bathroom and couldn't imagine how I would explain the current scene to them (or to the counsellor they might be forced to share it with at some point in the future). I found myself trying to hold my boxer shorts out of the way of the hair removal process, whilst trying to protect my vital parts from suffering chemical burns.

Eventually Lesley said she felt she had finished, realising that I had suffered enough and I admitted that I had learned a salutary lesson in some of the day to day difficulties women have to go through to meet the demands made on them by modern society.

I rinsed my legs, the sludgy mess almost blocking the plug hole, and looked at the results of my efforts or rather Lesley's efforts. I was reasonably pleased – not perfect by any means but my legs had been transformed from short, skinny and hairy, to short skinny and almost silky smooth. One of the many Tour de France goodies I had got was a set of temporary tattoos, so we completed our handiwork by applying one of those to my right calf. Wearing long trousers felt a little bit strange, but I found myself repeatedly running my hands along my newly smooth calves.

I was now as ready as I could have been. I had done my best to get in as many miles as I could over recent weeks, had eaten a reasonably sensible diet, had my bike serviced, bought my commemorative jersey and a couple of other unnecessary new things, and finally made my legs look as much like those of a seasoned professional as I could.

All I needed now was for the weather to be kind with sunny skies and a reasonable tail wind. In a couple of days' time I would be crossing the start line of the Tour de France and setting off toward Paris, where I would ride around the Arc de Triomphe, along the Champs Elysees and live a dream I had carried for as long as I could remember.

Stage 18
Grander than Grand

I still have an edition of 'The Harrogate Advertiser' which carries the headline 'Harrogate's Finest Hour'.

Even though I have lived in Harrogate for most of my adult life, I don't really know a lot about its history. I know it rose to prominence in Victorian times when visitors would come to make use of its mineral wells for their health giving properties, and that Agatha Christie turned up here, at what is now The Old Swan Hotel, after she disappeared in the nineteen twenties, because her husband had been having an affair. The twentieth century has meant that there is less faith in the value of consuming foul tasting water from the sulphur wells of the Turkish baths and the town has re-invented itself as a conference destination. Other than that, I think Harrogate has kept a reasonably modest profile, hosting annual flower shows and the agricultural Great Yorkshire Show, while quietly prospering and continuing to be a fine and pleasant place. The arrival of the Tour de France brought the town, briefly, to the attention of millions of people throughout the world. It may well be the biggest thing that has ever happened here. For once, I don't think the headline writers could be accused of getting over excited.

Thankfully, the morning of the day of Harrogate's 'finest hour' was dry. There had been a few spots of overnight rain, but the sun was breaking through the clouds and it looked as if the weather was only going to get better throughout the day.

Our plan was to cycle out to the village of Pool in Wharfedale, about ten miles outside Harrogate, about six miles into the route of the first stage. Then we would see the race pass, cycle back, get cleaned up and take our place outside Lesley's house, which was directly on the route and only about twelve hundred metres from the finish. We could watch the riders come past again and then run inside to see the final sprint on television.

There is a rule in cycling, formulated by a group of cyclists and on-line bloggers called the 'Velominati', which says that the correct number of bikes to own is $n + 1$, where 'n' is the number of bikes currently owned. It also says that the minimum number of bikes that should be owned is three, and that the maximum is $s-1$, when 's' is the number of bikes owned that would result in separation from your partner. Thanks to applying this rule to my own bike collection, it meant I could lend Scottish Lesley and Ian a bike each for the day, so after breakfast and time spent tweaking saddle heights and changing pedals, we were ready to set off to see the Tour. My brother Neil and my Dad joined us on bikes of their own.

Riding through town that morning felt almost surreal, the roads were so quiet. I had only ever seen them like this if I got up extra early for a summer club run, usually passing people staggering out of clubs and pubs after a long night out. Even though a lot of the roads weren't officially closed, there were hardly any cars. As we left town we joined a steady stream of cyclists, all heading in the same direction. The sun was out, and there was a fantastic atmosphere.

It was one of the most mixed pelotons that I have ever experienced – there weren't just Lycra clad club cyclists, but whole families riding together and bikes of every description, from old butcher's bikes to high end carbon fibre racers. Whoever they were and whatever bike they were riding, everyone had one common purpose and the feeling of sharing the same goal was almost palpable.

Before long, we rounded a bend and began to see the crowds who were gathering by the roadside. I paused for a moment to take it all in – the Tour de France was about to arrive in Yorkshire.

No matter how many times I said it to myself, it still seemed unreal.

The crowd was already a few deep, even though it was over two hours before the race was due, but we managed to get ourselves a good spot, when a lady very kindly let us lean our bikes against her house. We perched on a high wall which gave us a good view. The last few clouds had cleared away and the sun was out. Every so often an official vehicle of some kind would come past, resulting in excited cheers from everyone by the roadside. Police motorcyclists managed to get themselves the best reception, especially if they gave a 'high five' to the hundreds of outstretched children's hands.

The French police motorcycle riders who were escorting the Tour were welcomed liked celebrities at a film premier, they even stopped at various points so that people could have their photo taken with them.

The crowd got even more excited if any of the team cars came by, culminating in the biggest cheers of all as the first of the huge black Team Sky Jaguars came into view. Between all the episodes of excitement, there was an almost eerie quiet, until something else drew the attention of the crowd and the noise started again.

The race was due to make its official start at Harewood House at around noon and as the morning went on the excitement continued to build. Suddenly, without any warning there was a huge 'whoosh' as the Red Arrows acrobatic display team flew over in a tight arrow formation. There was a huge cheer, as everyone knew that the race would soon be here. The planes disappeared over the horizon and, seconds later, flew over the start line trailing red, white and blue smoke.

The tension rose and rose, helicopters began to buzz around above us, and more and more motorbikes and support cars came past. Then, huge cheers from a few hundred metres up the road, a couple more motorbikes, their engines drowned by the roar of the crowd and there they were – three leaders who had already broken away from the main peloton. Three men on bikes riding along a road I had ridden hundreds and hundreds of times. But these weren't just any three men on bikes, they were three Tour de France riders and I was seeing them for real. A few more support vehicles went past and then there was almost silence for a few moments as everyone strained their eyes up the road ready for the arrival of the rest of the race.

It was quite some time before more cars came through and another roar from amongst the crowd further along signalled that the main peloton was approaching. The huge multi coloured bunch streamed past in a blur, making it almost impossible to pick out any individual riders. The noise was a deafening mix of cheering, air horns, whistles and cow bells. The stream of official cars came next, getting just the same noisy reception as the cyclists. The long line of other accompanying cars, vans buses and motorbikes did nothing to dampen the enthusiasm of the crowd. Eventually, the road emptied, and there we were, a crowd of people standing in the sunshine, on an English summer's day in an English village. It suddenly seemed very quiet.

'It was worth coming just for that', said Scottish Lesley. We were lucky in that we were going to get to see the whole thing again later in the day. On most parts of the race's route, people wait at the roadside for hours and hours to see the race flash past, then have to wait until the roads re open before they can go home again and they only get the same thing we had just experienced. I understood how standing by the road side for hours would be worthwhile to see what we had just seen, but I was keen to set off towards Harrogate so we could re-live the whole experience.

The road back was one that I drive along regularly and it's usually busy. It hadn't been closed for the day but was empty of anything other than cyclists. It was a lovely feeling to be part of a streaming mass of thousands, in charge of the road and not feeling in the least bit vulnerable. As we neared Harrogate, we stopped at some traffic lights and were transfixed as a pair of red kites hovered in the air only a few feet above our heads.

The roads into Harrogate were all but empty, with hundreds of people walking towards where the finish was going to be. We wound our way back to my house and after getting changed set off to walk to Lesley's house to get ready for the finish.

Unable to get through on the mobile phone network, I had called Lesley on the land line to let her know we were on our way. She said that the crowds were already massive and that she had been told there was no way we could cross the road to get to her house. This meant a big diversion through the middle of town and around the masses of people.

This proved to be more of a challenge than we had anticipated. Although the rumours of three million visitors coming to Harrogate hadn't quite come true, there were an incredible number of people crammed into the town. Every street was packed almost solid and there was only enough room to allow very slow progress as we tried to make our way to Lesley's. She had gone home early, stocked up on supplies of pork pies (what else?), strawberries and champagne. She had moved her garden bench to the end of her driveway to stake a claim to an area of the footpath outside her house. Neighbours had further annexed bits of territory with deck chairs and stepladders.

The walk through town was proving to be the most stressful part of the day. Every road we turned down was jammed solid and police and stewards were doing their best to divert the crowds and keep everyone moving. Even though, as a local, I knew some short cuts, these were just as packed so didn't save us any time. I had felt the need to distinguish myself as a true cycling fan so was proudly wearing my Cappuccino Cycling Club celebratory t-shirt, and felt somehow disappointed that it didn't give me any magical powers or extra rights to get through the crowds any quicker than anyone else. Occasionally my phone would ring but each time I answered, it was cut off almost straight away, because the network was so overloaded, probably by people, like me, getting stressed at being held up, and ringing friends to ask, 'where the hell are you?'

It took us almost two hours to get to Lesley's – taking the shortest route in the absence of a global event taking place would have meant it should have taken about fifteen minutes. To add to our frustration, a crossing point had been opened up only a couple of hundred metres from where we were standing, which would have saved us a lot of stress. None of that mattered now, as we settled ourselves in, opened some drinks and tucked into the supply of pork pies and other delicacies.

It was just like it had been earlier in the day – the anticipation and excitement rising and rising, reaching fever pitch every time any type of vehicle came along. There was a huge round of applause and cheering as a bride and groom walked by. I can only imagine what the conversation must have been like when the poor couple realised that their own big day was going to clash with Harrogate's biggest day, and how much stress it must have added when they tried to work how just how they would get from the service to the reception.

We spent our time moving between our roadside vantage point and the television inside. Gareth's son Thomas was getting a bit bored, so we let him watch children's television while we carried on savouring the atmosphere outside. We took the precaution of putting the television remote control out of his reach – we didn't want to go in and find him asleep on top of it or having hidden it somewhere as the race reached its climax.

It was strange to watch the race unfold on familiar roads. As always, the coverage included a countdown of the remaining kilometres in the top corner of the screen. This was my usual point of reference if I was watching the end of a stage. Today was different – instead of thinking about how the riders had just past the fifty kilometres to go mark, I found myself thinking, 'Wow – there's Johnny Baghdad's' (the club's favourite stopping point in Masham), or 'ooh look – there's the garden centre!'

Eventually all the support cars shot past where we were standing and the cries of the crowd reached a crescendo, and the peloton came flying through. The road where we were standing is the sort of hill that can really make me struggle if I climb it at the end of a long ride, but the race shot past at an incredible speed, with Fabian Cancellara making an attempt at a late break for the line, pursued by Mark Cavendish's Omega Quick Step team, who were trying to set him up with victory. He had said earlier in the year that today was going to be the biggest day of his career so far – a pretty bold statement considering his list of achievements. Harrogate is his mum's home town and he spent a lot of time in the area when he was young. His mum was in the crowd, as were members of the royal family. The finish line was by a pub that had been renamed in his honour and if he could cross that line first, he would not only win the stage, but would be able to claim the yellow jersey of overall race leader, something he had never managed before.

As soon as the race had passed, we sprinted back into Lesley's house to see the finale on the television. The riders raced up Parliament Street, 'Look they're going past the Pump Rooms', and into the finishing straight. Just as they entered the last two hundred meters, they passed the Nationwide Building Society, Mark Cavendish tried to push his way past the Australian rider Simon Gerrans, and the result was that the two men's bikes tangled and they went sprawling and sliding across the tarmac, sending 'Cav' sliding all the way to just outside Betty's tearoom. This allowed Germany's Marcel Kittel to go on and win the sprint. From inside Lesley's house we could just hear the shouts of anguish from the huge crowd gathered over a kilometre away at the finish. I couldn't believe what I was seeing – we all jumped up and shouted at the television. The day had been perfect up until then. The weather had been kind, the television coverage had shown Yorkshire at its glorious best, the crowds had been huge, everyone had enjoyed a wonderful time. The final piece of the jigsaw seemed to go missing right at the last moment. 'Cav' had fallen. No win, no yellow jersey, no perfect end to a perfect day.

Cyclists, especially Tour de France cyclists, contrast massively from professional footballers in that the first thing they do after falling, or being brought down by someone else, is get up again. There's no such thing as 'injury time', and the more time they spend on the ground, the longer they have to struggle to catch up with everyone else. If they need medical treatment, they usually get this from the race doctor, who leans out of his car and tends to them as they ride along. The worrying thing about Mark

Cavendish, as he laid in the road outside Betty's tea rooms, was that it took him a long time to get up, when he did, he was holding his shoulder, usually a sign of a race ending broken collar bone. He did manage to re mount and ride one-handed across the finish line, but it was obvious that he was still in quite a lot of pain.

We sat in disbelief and watched the post-race analysis on television, which reported that Cavendish had been taken for x-rays, but that his injuries weren't thought to be too bad. The man he collided with, Simon Gerrans, who had also been sent sprawling, had appeared and said that although he had lost a fair bit of skin and had a few bruises, he would be taking the start the next day. Everyone was optimistic that Mark Cavendish would emerge from our local casualty department to say the same.

I woke early on the Sunday morning to the incredible prospect of the Tour de France passing my house. I still found this a very strange thing to contemplate. I had paid money in the past for the privilege of riding my bike on the same roads as the Tour, and now, as I leaned out of the side of my own bed, in my own house, in Yorkshire, I could see the route itself, simply by opening my curtains.

The sun was shining again and even though it was only about eight o'clock, there were already a few people in deck chairs at the side of the road. On any other Sunday, there would normally be a lot of traffic at this time, but today the road was silent.

I ran around the house like a child on Christmas morning, waking everyone up. We had a quick cup of tea and then set about making sure we had a good vantage point for later in the day. We carried garden furniture through the house and claimed a spot by the roadside. We spread ourselves out as much as we could with the addition of a few deckchairs. We hung a big Yorkshire flag from the tree and settled down for the morning. All around us, people were cooking bacon on barbecues for sandwiches and feasting from picnic tables. Just as on the day before, any vehicle that drove past got a huge cheer and most of the children seemed to be engaged in a competition to see who could get the most 'high fives' from police motorcyclists. Every so often, someone would ride by on a bike to huge cheers. Even Thomas developed a taste for such adulation and spent much of the morning riding past us time after time on his little mountain bike, soaking up the applause.

I was slightly disappointed with my haul form the publicity caravan. I only managed a cotton polka dot cap and a sachet of dairy free energy gel. Even so, it was a lot of fun to see all the floats and cheer at the people on them. They all still looked happy and fresh faced, and obviously were yet to tire of having to spend all day smiling and waving. I wondered if they would look any different by the time they reached Paris.

By this time, the news had come through that Mark Cavendish wouldn't be taking the start. His shoulder injury was too bad to cope with three weeks of racing so he had appeared on television announcing his retirement from the event. He also had the good grace to say that the crash had been his fault and that he had apologised to Simon Gerrans, who had also fallen at the same time as he had. I can't imagine how disappointed he must have felt. He had probably thought (like almost everyone else) that he would have spent this day riding through his mother's home town wearing the yellow jersey. Had it happened, it would have been like something out of the sort of story that would be dismissed as being too good to be true, which had unfortunately turned out to be the case.

We spent our time between our roadside table and the television in the house. The stage started in York and would pass my house less than an hour later. Again, it wasn't like watching a global event, because every landmark the race passed was a familiar one – roundabouts and junctions that I either drive or cycle across almost every day. The crowds were huge. The centre of York looked packed and even the tower of the Minster had a yellow banner and its own religious French pun ('Allez – lujah) draped over it.

Once the television coverage reached Knaresborough, less than four miles away, we got ourselves back outside for the final time, ready to see the race. It was over two years since the announcement that the Tour was coming to Yorkshire and the realisation that it would pass my house. Two years of excitement, anticipation and trying to imagine what this would be like.

In a little over twenty seconds it was over. The riders streamed past and I managed to pick out Jens Voigt, in the polka dot jersey he had won the day before. I spotted a few of the Team Sky riders and the yellow jersey of Marcel Kittel. The bunch went by so quickly it was impossible to take anything else in.

The team cars followed, and then more press and support vehicles. In a few moments, the road was quiet. That was it. Millions of people the world over would still have one eye on their televisions, watching the stage unfold, just as they do every year, some of them hoping that one day they might be lucky enough to see it for real. To them, this was just like last year and the year before, an early stage of the Tour when the riders start to find their legs and the overall contenders are happy to keep themselves out of trouble.

For me and for almost the entire population of Yorkshire it wasn't like that at all. We had just experienced a piece of local history, something that everyone who was there would always remember. It was Yorkshire's own 'Kennedy moment' the moment when everyone would be able to say what they were doing on the day the Tour came past. It was bigger than if Wimbledon had been staged at the local tennis club, bigger than if the football world cup final been held Harrogate Town's ground. Bigger and about as likely to happen, except that it had happened. The Tour had come past my house. I still couldn't quite believe it.

The crowds of people slowly thinned and faded away. A couple of hours later, the traffic had returned to the roads of Harrogate. We walked with Scottish Lesley and Ian to see them off on their journey back to Scotland and then had a quiet beer outside the pub in the station. We sat and watched the world go by.

'Fancy another one?' asked Lesley, as I finished my pint of 'Pedal on' pale ale.

'No thanks', I said. 'I want to get home – the Tour's on the telly'

And so, hand in hand, we walked home, through town. It was

like any other Sunday. It didn't seem as if anything massive had happened. Harrogate looked and felt its usual self. Here and there were yellow bikes and bunting fluttering in the summer breeze, but the bars and cafés were back to serving regulars and tomorrow was just another Monday.

The Tour de France had been and gone. Over the next three weeks, many more towns would have their own special day, but none of them would be quite as special as this one. It had truly been the grandest of Grand Departs.

Stage 19
Start to Finish

On most of the mornings when I get up early to set off for a club run, the routine is similar. I get up as quietly as I can, eat a good breakfast, fill up my bottles, say goodbye to anyone in the house, and go to meet my club mates.

This time it felt strange to go through exactly the same routine and set off on my bike just as if I was going out for a quick spin. I rode through town just as I would normally but instead of heading for our usual meeting place outside a school, I made my way to the Prologue Performance Cycling Café to join an excited group of club mates and have a quick pre-ride espresso. I didn't particularly need or want one but having a coffee, just like the professionals do before every stage, just seemed like the right thing to do.

We had agreed to leave at eight-thirty and as the time approached poor Jonathan was starting to feel the stress of being the person who had come up with the whole idea in the first place. It was understandable – people were chatting, drinking coffee and relaxing with no sense of urgency. Some were even carrying out last minute tyre changes, which really should have been done the night before. Inevitably, at least two mature, sensible and intelligent adults had mislaid passports or wallets and were somehow managing to make Jonathan feel as if he should help them find them. He turned to me totally exasperated and said, 'Fuck me Martin, it's like herding cats!'

Eventually after more swearing and a few calls to order we lined up for a photo in front of the shop then set off toward

Harewood in one big group. It was a beautiful sunny day with only a slight breeze. A perfect day to be out on a bike, made even better by the thought of our final destination.

It didn't take long to get to the gates of Harewood House for a few more photos before we formed into smaller groups and set off towards Hull.

Everyone knew that with three long days in the saddle we would have to ride sensibly and make sure we worked together as much as possible. There were far too many of us to ride in one group. For the sake of our own safety and the sanity of any motorist who would need to get past us as we made our way to Hull, we split up into groups of seven or eight riders.

I was busy doing yet another reorganisation of the gels and various bits and pieces in my back pockets when I heard my name being called from across the road. 'Martin – over here, come on!' It was Martin Procter, the club's road captain and an ideal riding partner thanks to his experience and patient nature. He was next to Jonathan, who, as ride organiser had the definitive route in his handlebar mounted GPS unit. Jonathan's dad was also driving one of the support vans, so I took advantage of the potential for any bias in the way the pork pies might be given out and scooted over to join them.

The rest of the group was made up of Jason, who was known as the club poster boy because his image appears in moody black and white print above the fire place in the Prologue café, Bernie, one of the strongest riders taking part and Stuart, who had had to cram his training after recovering from his leaf induced somersault. The other two riders I was joining were Dave, who had had the cheek to come on the fixed wheel century ride on a bike with gears, and Charlie. Charlie was only along for the first part of the ride, excusing himself from coming all the way to Paris because he had made the mistake of arranging his wedding on the same weekend as the finish of the Tour de France.

Jonathan had arranged for the support vans to stop at strategic points along the way so that we could refill our water bottles and have something to eat. His dad had spent evening after evening baking flap jack, which was supplemented by boxes of sausage rolls, cakes, cold cans of pop and of course, pork pies. In my own mind, I convinced myself that regular meetings with the van meant that instead of doing one really long ride, I was doing several short ones with plenty of pork pie breaks in between.

We soon got into the routine of riding as a group – rotating regularly so that we would spend about ten minutes on the front and about half an hour riding sheltered by someone else, as well as having someone different to talk to each time the call of 'change' rang out.

Our first stop was in York – a huge and rather early refill of various pork based energy made up of bacon and sausage sandwiches washed down with tea and finished off with cake. As we rode towards Hull the roads started to bring back memories of days with Dicco and how we used to pretend these roads would lead us to Paris. This time, despite Dicco's absence, that really was the case. We rode into the village of Holme on Spalding Moor to meet the van for the first time, a place I remembered well from passing through there on many Hull Thursday Road Club outings.

The last leg of the day took us into Hull, past West Park where I remembered racing in school boy circuit races. We passed Cliff Pratt's bike shop, still open after all the years since Dicco and I used to hang around there trying to show off.

Once we got to the docks we were reunited with the other groups before loading our bikes onto the van ready to board the ferry. First stop, obviously, was the bar for a bit of rehydration, then off to our cabins to freshen up in time for our evening meal.

The meal was an 'all you can eat' buffet – perfect for a bunch of hungry middle aged cyclists determined to fill up with as much carbohydrate as is physically possible. There were some interesting combinations – plates containing everything from roast beef and Yorkshire pudding to Chinese chicken, chips, roast potatoes, noodles and pasta, usually on the same plate at the same time.

Suitably stuffed full to the point of barely being able to sit comfortably, we returned to the bar to wash down our meal. The ferry company had tried to make the overnight crossing into a kind of mini-cruise, with live entertainment laid on. To be fair, you can hardly expect someone with a vast amount of talent to spend night after night performing to audiences largely made up of tipsy coach passengers and drunken stag parties, so we didn't spend too long listening to versions of classic songs being, at best, 'reinterpreted in a way the original artist could never have imagined'.

We were all tired from our first day's eighty five mile ride, so we didn't have to suffer the 'artistes' for too long before going to bed. Back at my cabin, I carefully hung up my kit for the following day and fell asleep after managing to read only a few lines of my book. (Predictably, it was a book about cycling, in this case 'Gironimo' by Tim Moore).

The next morning saw our second assault on the buffet. This was another opportunity for us to stuff ourselves with carbohydrates for the day ahead. I remember when I worked as a nurse seeing vats of porridge arrive at the ward each morning – it would have been slowly simmered for hours so that it reached a creamy consistency suitable for even the frailest and most toothless of elderly mouths to be able to take in its goodness. The stuff that was on the breakfast buffet of the ferry looked very similar and it went down a treat – loaded with sugar and honey. This was followed by piles of bacon, toast, beans and pancakes, and cup after cup of strong tea.

Understandably, the roads that lead out of the port of Zebrugge and on into Belgium are designed to ensure the quick exit of lorries and caravan-towing Volvos, rather than groups of nervous cyclists. We rode as one big group again until the roads started to feel a bit safer, before a brief comfort break gave us time to reform into the same groups as we had been in the day before.

We often view other countries as endlessly beautiful, forgetting that as tourists, we only visit the best bits of the rest of the world. It's easy to forget that for every stunning European city, there are as many, if not more, grim industrial towns and dull rural landscapes. This was where we were now. The scenery was about as far removed from the Europe we see in travel brochures as it was possible to be. Many of the villages had a bleak and depressed air about them, and seemed almost deserted with shuttered windows and empty looking businesses.

The tree lined roads were often ram rod straight – heading toward the horizon like a scene from a road movie. Thankfully, we were lucky enough to be enjoying sunshine and something of a tail wind, which was helping us make rapid progress. It can be soul destroying riding a bike into a strong headwind, especially along a dead straight road in a featureless landscape. We were all thankful that the wind stayed at our backs, and the sun kept on shining. Riding into a wind, soaked by rain on those types of road would have been a drastically different experience to the sheer pleasure we were enjoying.

We did pass through some pretty places. One of which had a beautiful cobbled main street which we hammered down at full pelt. This was our first experience of the cobbles that make cycling in this area so famous. We flew along them as fast as we could, trying our best to enjoy the experience. In reality, it felt like we were being shaken to bits. The result was that Bernie's chain was thrown off with such force that he had to take it apart to untangle it.

Jonathan had planned the route to pay the occasional homage to the area we were in. We headed towards Roubaix so that we could ride a few laps of the famous Velodrome. It was early afternoon when we reached the outskirts of the town and we were getting hungry. The fuel reserves provided by the unlimited buffet on the ferry were long gone. Whilst it's usually true to say that 'two heads are better than one', it may be just as true to say that 'seven heads are a lot worse than two'. Once we had found the road that led to the Velodrome, we couldn't really decide between us whether to head for lunch or go and pay our respects with a few symbolic laps of the famous track. It didn't help that having decided to go for lunch we then changed our minds and got a bit lost trying to retrace our route.

Arriving back at the Velodrome we saw that the gate onto the track was open and there were a few people having picnics and playing on the grass in the middle, as well as a child of about three who was riding around the banking on a little scooter.

I had been here before of course, but hadn't realised at the time how tatty the place was. This was a place that most cyclists held an almost religious attachment to, a shrine to thousands and thousands of dreamers. In reality, it's a bit of a let-down. This holy site is just a run-down municipal sports stadium that is open during the day to any wannabe cyclist to ride the famous banking. Judging by much of the litter that was blowing around in the wind it looked like the teenage population of Roubaix made pretty good use of it at night too, as somewhere to drink cider and explore the lumpy bits of each other's bodies.

After a few photos and fake victory salutes along the finishing straight, we realised that we really had to get something to eat. There was still a long way to go to Cambrai, where we would be spending the night. We found our way to the square and met up with the other group who were just finishing their lunch. We ordered a round of drinks and when they arrived asked to see the menu. With a Gallic shrug that was obvious enough to be a cliché, the waiter said 'Sorry Monsieur, the kitchen is finished'. He wasn't the least bit moved by the look of utter horror on our faces, the chef had finished and gone, so there was nothing he could do.

Thankfully, one of our club mates who had managed to beat the deadline for ordering lunch said that he had seen a nice bakery near where the support vans were parked. He gleefully pointed out that although it wouldn't be as good or as filling as the 'delicious and amazing' toasted sandwich he had just enjoyed, we would at least be able to get something to eat. Distraught and hungry we headed off in search of some form of nourishment. It didn't take us long to find the van. On the footpath opposite where it was parked was a young man in a track suit, sat on a plastic chair outside his own pizza take away shop. He was whiling away the day by smoking, wolf whistling at women and chatting up almost every young girl whose attention he could gain as they walked past. He seemed pleased to become our saviour and to have something else to do as we ordered seven fourteen inch pizzas which we dispatched in the time it usually takes to eat a small sandwich. He made himself even more popular by giving us a few bottles of free fizzy orange with which to wash them down.

In all the bits of advice I have ever read about the nutritional needs of a long distance cyclist, I don't think I have ever seen take away pizza being recommended. Judging by the way we rode the next few miles, I began to think that someone, somewhere had been missing something when it came to advice about what athletes should eat. I don't know the calorific or carbohydrate make-up of the pizzas we ate but, whatever it was, it gave us plenty of energy and we seemed to fly along almost effortlessly. The constant swish of wheels and the occasional call to change places became the only sound I was aware of. Every so often Jonathan would shout out to tell us that we had just done another five miles in around twelve minutes, which meant that the combination of close group riding, a bit of a tailwind and a belly full of pizza meant I got the closest I ever had to the age old target of covering twenty five miles in less than an hour.

In another piece of masterful organisation, Jonathan had planned the route so that we could ride a section of the cobbles that make up part of the Paris-Roubaix race route. Not wanting to do things in short measure, he had chosen the famous Arenberg forest section, thus making sure that we got as much of an experience as possible.

The seven of us took turns to ride a short section of the vicious cobbles, just to get a feel of the experience and as a photo opportunity. As soon as I had done my bit for the camera, I made use of the cycle path that had been denied to me the last time I was here.

We gathered together at the end of the cobbles for a while and had a bite to eat. As we stood there in the sunshine, it felt a very peaceful place, in total contrast to how it must be on the day the race comes through and to the hellish world of the mine below us. There was a small memorial to Jean Stablinski who after working under the ground where we stood, had then raced down this stretch of road long before I was even born.

The day was wearing on and we needed to meet the support van. The heat and the type of thirst that can only be brought on by practically inhaling a fourteen inch pizza, then riding hard for a couple of hours, meant we were running out of water.

Unfortunately, we couldn't find the van. After a few phone calls we found out that it had been pressed into service to take Peter Hooren, who was in one of the other groups, to the local casualty department with a suspected broken collar bone – by far the most common injury to befall cyclists. The diagnosis had been confirmed by the time we met him at the hotel that night. No one really knew what to say. The fact that it is a relatively minor and non-life threatening injury is little comfort to someone who has spent all year trying to get fit for such an epic ride, only to have it all ruined in one brief moment.

Despite heat and thirst we carried on, feeling pretty happy. We had been told that there is a fresh water tap in every graveyard in France and we were pretty sure we could take advantage of this if we had to. As the afternoon wore on we came to a village and pulled up outside the local supermarket. We decided the best plan was to buy some water and fill up our bottles enough to last through the last bit of the day. We took the chance to splash out an extra two Euros between us to buy a box of ice lollies.

There are some unexpected moments in life which just seem perfect. As we sat eating our ice lollies, seven grown men enjoying childish treats, it felt very much like one of those moments. We knew we were not too far from the end of the day's ride and none of us felt too exhausted. After a few minutes, one of the other groups came past. At the back was Harry, as he looked at us we could all see his tongue hanging out and he almost looked to be pleading with us. I have never seen anyone look so jealous or so desperate to stop for an ice lolly but he had to put in a sprint as his group sped on with a few jeers and a wave.

It was early evening when we rolled up the drive of our hotel on the outskirts of Cambrai. We parked our bikes and set about a bit of post ride refreshment consisting of cold beer and salty nibbles, which felt like a perfect combination. I'm sure that the last things any of the professionals in the Tour are allowed at such times are salty snacks and beer, they probably have to make do with a recovery drink and a massage. I know which I'd prefer, and whatever is in a recovery drink or how magical the hands of a masseur might be, they would not have made me feel any better than those two cold beers and handfuls of salty baked miniature biscuits.

Jonathan's planning skills and forethought were demonstrated once again at the evening meal when he produced a copy of the menu we had all filled in before we left home, allowing the harassed staff to give everyone the right meal and letting us all satisfy our hunger without any delay. I'm too old to be able to stay up late two nights in a row, never mind after two long days of cycling, so it was only a couple of beers later before I was in my room readying another set of kit for the last day into Paris.

Like many men of my age, I had spent a small part of my childhood as a cub scout. Apart from memories of a leader who used to sit at the front of the hall screaming at an unruly bunch of boys to do as she instructed, whilst smoking her way through at least half a packet of cigarettes during each meeting, the motto, 'be prepared' has stayed with me.

Porridge has never caught on across the continent so I had 'been prepared' by bringing a couple of pots of instant porridge with me. I sneaked it into breakfast the next morning and used the hot water fountain that was meant for our coffee to get it ready. It wasn't as good as the porridge I had enjoyed on the ferry but it made an ideal starter, before I piled my plate with croissants and baguettes to add to my body's carbohydrate stores, ready for our last day. Because it was early and I was tired, breakfast felt like a chore; it was hard to force myself to eat as much as I knew I needed to.

Leaving Cambrai and setting off for our final day in Paris, I couldn't help but wonder how I would have been feeling if I'd been doing this every day for three weeks, rather than for three days. I have heard of riders in the Tour who say that they get stronger in the first part of the race, before the fatigue sets in as they get towards the finish in Paris. I was quite relieved that I felt as good as I did and that I'd managed to contribute to our group so far.

It was very humid in the early part of the day and we seemed to spend an age passing through sleepy villages and across a largely featureless agricultural landscape. We passed lots of signs telling us to expect 'Gravillons', which meant that we were constantly bothered by loose chippings which stung our legs and threatened to work their way into our tyres. The slick organisation we had enjoyed so far almost led to us asking Jonathan why he hadn't warned the local council to postpone their road resurfacing program until after we had passed through the area.

As we made our way South we were joined by a group of French cyclists who were on their way to Nice. They looked very slick, in matching team jerseys and all astride extremely expensive looking bikes. As they drew level I used my best schoolboy French to have a chat with one of them. I like to think I told him that we were a club from the town where the first stage of the Tour had finished and that we were on our way to see the finish in Paris. How much of this was lost in the translation and drowned out by the wind, I will never know.

They were a fit looking bunch, something that was proven as one of them passed us, riding non-handed as we went uphill. I wondered if he had read the same fitness advice as I had all those years ago or if he was just trying to show off. Then I realised he was taking a picture on his phone. He had been particularly complementary about our commemorative jerseys, unfortunately he and his friends were obviously so impressed by the back of our outfits that they didn't want to spoil the view by taking a turn at the front, because they sat resolutely in our slipstream until they turned off and left us to ourselves.

As the day went on the places we passed through started to seem much more prosperous and well kept. The terrain became noticeably hillier, with rolling green fields replacing the barren flatness of the route so far. The greyness from our early start had been replaced with bright sunshine and we continued to be blessed with a tail wind. Unfortunately, the support van was engaged in dealing with a problem in one of the other groups so once again we found ourselves short of food and drinks and keeping an eye out for a handily placed cemetery with a its promise of a supply of fresh water.

Even though we were hungry and thirsty our spirits remained high – we rode on, taking our turns and enjoying the scenery and weather while looking forward to getting to Paris. By the time we reached Liancourt we had covered eighty four miles, meaning my self-deluding idea of 'a few short rides with plenty of stops for cake and pork pie' had proven to be wholly unrealistic.

It would be fair to say that Liancourt has the air of a place that had seen better days. Its steep main street led to a square that was all but deserted, full of tatty looking empty shops. Luckily, about half way up the same hill we had just climbed was a small pizza restaurant which was about the only place showing any sign of life. Having benefited so much from eating pizza the day before, the fact that the restaurant was open and willing to accept a group of sweaty middle aged men made it the perfect choice and no one seemed to want to try looking to see if Liancourt had anything else to offer. Being so close to the end of the ride meant that we were starting to feel just a little bit celebratory, so we all treated ourselves to a small beer before ordering our food. Just like in the square in Roubaix, we ate the pizzas much more quickly than anyone normally would and after a few more drinks of full fat, high sugar, energy filled fizzy pop we got onto our bikes for the final ride into Paris.

As we left the village, the road rose steeply up a short hill and I suffered a case of 'café legs' as my legs suddenly felt as heavy as lead. It took a few miles before they warmed up and I felt comfortable again.

I thought back to when Lesley and I had spent a weekend in Paris earlier in the year. We'd wandered around the city aimlessly, ridden around on Segways and had even climbed to the top of the Arc de Triomphe and looked down the length of the Champs Elysees, where I had spent more than a few moments thinking about the day when I'd ride its length having cycled all the way there from home. On the last day of our trip we went to the cathedral of the Sacre Coeur and gazed at the city laid out before us. It seemed fitting that the first definite sighting of the city of Paris I saw from my bike was the Sacre Couer – rising above the distant horizon before the whole of the city itself came into view.

By now I was starting to struggle – I knew when I joined the 'three day fast' group that I was going to be in the company of riders who were fitter than me. Even though I had enjoyed the challenge, there was a sense of relief as well as delight as we got closer and closer to our goal. The last bit of the ride was exciting and scary in equal measure – the bits on dual carriageway being a bit scary, whilst the bits in between were exciting. Finally we rolled down a short hill and spotted the support van parked in a small square. Across the road from it was a bar, and there in the sunshine were a few of our club mates. It was a wonderfully happy reunion, especially for Jonathan as he met up with Sarah who had been part of the four day group. We celebrated with the by now inevitable couple of very cold beers and very salty snacks, the snacks being given free no doubt with the intention that their saltiness would result in making us thirsty enough to order just one more beer, maybe two.

We really didn't have time to linger and the barman generously filled all our bottles with water and ice before we set off through the suburbs towards the park where we would be reuntied with everyone else.

There are frequent charity bike rides that start in the UK – usually in London and end in the middle of Paris. Because of this, there are plenty of fluorescent orange arrows fixed to signposts that direct cyclists into the middle of the city, so we decided to follow those. Part of Jonathan's organisational plan had been programming GPS units with the route he had mapped. This had worked amazingly well so far. Every so often, as we rode through a deserted part of rural France he would shout something like 'off to the right up ahead', as if by magic, a right turn or sometimes just a sharp bend in the road, would appear and we would know we were on the right route. In three days of cycling across three countries on unfamiliar roads, the only time we had gone wrong was when we rode past the entrance to our hotel in Cambrai the night before, even then we had only added about twenty metres to our total for the day.

The trouble was that the orange arrows and Jonathan's GPS didn't always agree and he was pretty vocal about it. It was understandable – he had spent long hours in planning, downloading and checking our route and here we were, ignoring him and behaving like a bunch of over excited school children on a trip to a sweet factory. Our way of thanking him, in usual club fashion, was to tease him until he went quiet and eventually, the route on his GPS and the little orange markers started to agree more than disagree and he seemed to cheer up a bit.

The whole plan was to end in a reunion of the three and four day groups in the Parc de Monceau, then on to the Champs Elysees for the grand finale of our ride. The joint guidance system of Jonathan's GPS unit and the fluorescent orange arrows soon directed us to the entrance with its ornate gates. Parisians were promenading in the early evening sunshine and there were hundreds of tourists relaxing and eating ice creams. In the middle of it all, sprawled around the grass verges and surrounded by their bikes were the members of the four day group, who gave us a round of applause as we went to join them. After a short while the rest of the three day riders joined us and we were ready for the final part of our journey – a dream come true moment when we would ride along the Champs Elysees.

Obviously the Champs Elysees is a major road through a capital city – not the sort of road that is ideal for cyclists. Add to this the fact that there were over forty of us, one of whom was determined to ride with his newly broken collar bone and all the ingredients were there for anything between comedy and catastrophe. We needed a plan that would ensure our safety, and protect the motorists of Paris from having a squashed English cyclist on their conscience.

We decided between us that we should make use of the

support vans as a kind of mobile protective barrier. The idea was that there would be one van in front, followed by a column of Cappuccino Cycling Club members, behind which would be another van, ensuring that we were as highly visible as possible. The plan worked perfectly – for about ten metres.

Just as we set off, a glamorous Parisian lady decided that she needed to get her Renault Clio into her driveway, which unfortunately was positioned about half way along the line of Cappuccino riders. We had to let her through, and this meant that the lead van, plus about a dozen riders, had left the rest of the group behind. A fair bit of shouting and waving brought things back as planned and we were soon at the huge roundabout where stands the Arc de Triomphe. The great moment when I would get to ride my bike down one of the world's most iconic roads was now only seconds away. I could feel a huge surge of emotion coming over me.

The whole group rode proudly onto the famous roundabout in tight formation, following the lead van which was heading, or so we thought, for the Champs Elysees exit. One of the support team, Bradley, was leaning out of the window trying to capture the moment on video and grinning wildly. As the van left the roundabout someone noticed that it was leaving via the wrong exit. As Bradley realised the reason we were all screaming at him, his expression changed to a look of horror before he disappeared inside the cab to redirect Richard, who was driving. The sensible thing to do would have been to carry on down the wrong road before regrouping and turning around, but instead we looked on in disbelief as the van made a u-turn and re-entered the roundabout, followed by a weaving column of cyclists. Richard must have been confused by all the over excitement and left the roundabout again at the next exit. It was still the wrong one and the screaming and shouting scenario was repeated, followed by another u-turn back into the traffic. As he was obviously unsure of which way to go, and was understandably distracted by being shouted at, he took a much more cautious approach from then on – he simply did another lap to give himself time to get it right. By this point we had the whole roundabout to ourselves. I can only assume that the locals had been forced to stop either through terror, or having to dry their eyes from laughing so much. So we had the privilege of doing a full circuit of a traffic free Arc de Triomphe before we rode delightedly onto the Champs Elysees.

It was just the sort of evening that comes to mind if you try to conjure up a mental picture of what you think Paris should be like. The busy bars looked to be full of glamorous people, sipping drinks and enjoying the sunshine. We were just about managing to stay together as a group and appreciate it all. Almost every bar we passed was full of drinkers who gave us shouts of encouragement, and some even gave us applause, answered by appreciative waves and the sound of the horns of the support vans.

I had always tried to imagine what it must be like for a professional cyclist to ride down the cobbles of the Champs Elysees after completing three weeks of the Tour de France. They must have so many mixed emotions – a sense of satisfaction at having lasted the distance, of achievement if they've done well. The crowds must give them an extra rush of adrenaline to help them over the last few miles, and they must wonder what it will be like the next day – to not have to get up and start racing for the first time three weeks. Although I can't pretend I'd earned the right to feel anything like the professionals felt, I still experienced every one of those feelings.

I had lived this moment in my imagination thousands of times since I had first changed my mind about getting a Raleigh Chopper and chosen a 'racer' instead. The difference was that this time, the trees that shaded my back really were on the Champs Elysees, and not lining the road towards Beverley as I rode with Dicco to meet Hull Thursday Road Club for a Sunday run out. This time, I really was going to cross the finish line of the Tour de France. It hadn't taken me three weeks to get here like I had imagined it would. I wasn't wearing the yellow jersey, I wasn't making history. I had dreamed of this ever since I first saw those grainy images of the Tour de France on television, ever since Dicco and I had nervously turned up at our first club run. That was when I had turned the pedals on the start of a journey that would lead me to where I was now.

In so many ways, the reality of that moment was as far removed from those dreams as it could possibly have been, the route I had followed was different, but ultimately, the destination was the same.

From start to finish, from Leeds to Paris, the end of a journey, but not the end of the road.

Epilogue
Twenty-One Hairpins

It had been a much harder day than I could have possibly imagined. Despite all the warnings from everyone with a scrap of knowledge about riding a bike, I was still more exhausted than I ever thought I would be. Far more exhausted than I ever thought possible.

I had reached the final feed station in Bourg d'Oisans, at the foot of the greatest temple of them all. All the false flats were over, the little hills were passed but at least I knew the broom wagon was still out of sight. There was no stopping me now. For the second time in my life I was going to complete a stage of the Tour de France and this time it had all the glamour and cachet I had ever dreamed of. I was at the foot of Alpe d'Huez, and there was a crowd of spectators waiting to see me to the top. Twenty-one hairpin bends between me and my ultimate boyhood dream.

I laid my bike against a post and went over to see what was left on the tables of free food and drink that had been laid out for the riders. Had I been a pro of course, I would merely have had to pedalled past while a helper handed me a bag of goodies to stuff into my jersey pockets before throwing the bag to a thankful fan at the roadside who would have gone away with the best Tour souvenir of all. I grabbed some dried out malt loaf, a couple of bananas and, best of all, a couple of bottles of blue coloured mineral water. At the time, blue mineral water seemed an entirely natural thing. It was only as I started to pour them into my water bottles that I realised I had picked up peppermint cordial. I tried drinking some of it, but the heat of the day had warmed it up, it was like drinking warm toothpaste. I threw it away and went and got one of the bottles of yellow mineral water. Much better – lemon and lime but fizzy, which isn't ideal when you feel like you are about to explode. I gulped as much as I could and kneeled by my bike to put the rest into my bottles. Probably another bad move – fizzy water when I couldn't resist the temptation to drink and drink.

As I looked up I saw someone pointing a TV camera at me. I just stared blankly at him. Back in my school days I longed to be filmed climbing this very mountain. I had imagined that the film would show me staring into the eyes of my rival before accelerating off into the distance, leaving him shocked and struggling in my wake. Instead, I looked shattered, had a half eaten energy bar smeared down my shorts and was on my knees in a car park.

As I got back on my bike I couldn't believe how much my body hurt. There were quite a few people by the side of the road shouting encouragement as I pedalled away. Finally the mountain came into view. Twenty one hairpins and I would have done it. I set myself a target – at least three before I had a drink. I became aware of a hissing sound. 'Bollocks! Not now'. I looked at my tyres to see which one was punctured, but they both looked OK. I couldn't understand it. I kept looking down, again and again, before my frazzled brain registered the fact that the hissing was coming from the fizzy water in my bottles. I took another huge gulp. Half a bottle gone and I was only at the start of the climb. Along with the water I had also swallowed all the fizz – it had to escape somehow – the resulting belch scared me.

My intention to get to the third hairpin before I had a drink was already proving to be about as realistic an ambition as actually going the whole hog and saying I could win the Tour. I'd read countless times that the first part of Alpe d'Huez is the hardest. I crawled my way to the first corner, passing countless people who were already pushing their bikes and countless more lying on the concrete wall by the side of the road or in the small amount of shade. On any normal day, the sight of a middle aged man lying at the side of the road would have had me pulling over in a panic, mobile phone in one hand already dialling the emergency services. In this case, I couldn't even think about that, my eyes were fixed on the hairpin up ahead. Anyway, a whole fleet of ambulances wouldn't have been able to cope with the countless prone forms scattered along the road.

It became obvious that I wasn't going to get to the top without stopping (another equally realistic idea began to from in my mind – 'Why don't I win the Tour and play for England in the World Cup final?). This was horrendous in a way that was outside anything I could have imagined.

The whole climb became like an out of body experience. At one point I convinced myself that once I'd got around the next bend, I'd be in the shade. It was days later when I finally understood that the only way I'd have been in the shade would have been if I was on the other side of the mountain, but the road doesn't go *round* the mountain – it winds its way up one side. At four o'clock on a July afternoon it's the side that's in full sun. Nice if you're in a cafe enjoying a cool beer, dreadful if you're forty and trying to ride up it on a bike.

I struggled on. I had to stop more times than I can remember or care to admit to. I remember reading once that Lance Armstrong had to use his brakes a few times when going up a mountain because he and his team mates were going so quickly that they couldn't rely on gravity to slow them down enough to get around the hairpins. Well Lance, I've got news for you, you might have used your brakes a couple of times going up Alpe d'Huez, but I had to use mine a whole heap of times. Gravity wasn't the problem; the truth was that I kept having to stop because I thought I was going to be sick.

At one point I realised that whilst I was off the bike I may as well walk a bit instead of just sitting there, so I did that. At one hairpin I stopped to rest and a few metres ahead someone had set up a garden sprinkler to spray water out across the road. I rode through it to gain some of its coolness, but remember saying out loud, 'Actually that's not very nice'.

Further up still – the view was stunning but I barely noticed it, I came across an Englishman pushing an old steel bike. I talked to him for a while. He was in tears. Not just about the fact that he was suffering so much, but the fact that he had another week to go before he went home. He was on an organised trip that took in the chance to see a couple of stages of the real Tour, yet what he really wanted at that moment in time was to go home. Probably to his mum, to lay on a sofa, read comics and be fed jam sandwiches, just like when you're poorly as a child and you get to stay off school for the day and be made a fuss of.

Once all the fizzy water was gone, I had to fight my way through a crowd to fill my bottles from a stream at the side of the road. It was every man for himself. There was no 'After you mate' here, just elbows and hard stares, and more great gulping mouthfuls of ice cold water to add to the chaos that seemed to be taking place in my stomach.

I passed the village sign for Huez, and counted down the hairpins. Each one is numbered, which can either seem like a blessing or extreme psychological torture, depending on your mental state at the time.

Finally, the village proper came into view. By this point there were riders coming down the hill towards me, having done their ride for the day. Sometimes they came a few at a time, but I just ignored them and let *them* avoid *me*. 'You lot are having a laugh if you think I'm getting out of your way', I thought or words to that effect.

At last the road began to level off and I started to feel better. Then, surely, the most bizarre and vivid hallucination of all. Standing by the road was a stunning blond girl, with long slim legs. She was wearing a tight vest and khaki hot pants. She looked like Kylie Minogue. She shouted, 'You're all amazing, absolutely bloody amazing'. As I passed her I looked over my shoulder because I really couldn't believe what I was seeing, but this just made we weave and wobble around so much that I was at risk of falling, so I fixed my eyes on the road ahead and carried on. I asked somebody later – they had seen her too. I can't imagine how long she must have stood there or what could have made her want to spend a day watching thousands of middle aged men struggle up a mountain on their bikes.

Then, the road dropped down a little and I could hear the public address system at the finish. I rounded the last corner and sprinted as hard as I could for the line. I faded badly with about a hundred metres still to go, and just managed to raise one arm as I finally crossed the finish line. I stopped and exhausted, leaned on the handlebars, an official bent down at my side to take the timer off my ankle. I looked down at him and tried to concentrate on not being sick on his head. Once he was out of the way, an even braver lady came over, gave me a kiss on the cheek, then handed me a medal and a bag of food. I set off to find my way to the cable car that was supposed to have been organised for our trip down the mountain to our hotel.

As I scrambled up the steps to the cable car, a man told me it was closed. I could see that there were still gondolas moving, so the machinery was obviously still operating and I was desperate to get back down the mountain. By this time there were a few of us, so by sheer weight of numbers and by some fairly aggressive waving of bikes, we pushed past him and got into the next gondola before he could stop us. It seemed a spectacular oversight on the part of the organisers, for them to organise for eight thousand people to ride up a mountain, but not think it necessary to ask the chap running the cable car to do a bit of overtime to help get everyone back down again.

The hotel was equally accommodating. No one on reception, and an extra charge for towels. Then corridors and stairwells lit by the sort of timing devices that guarantee to plunge you into darkness before you reach your room. Couple this with the fact that I was trying to carry my bag and my bike and soon, for the first time since that rainy day under a shop awning in Hawes, and probably for only about the third time in my entire life, I ran out of expletives. By the time I got to my room all the pain of the day's efforts had paled into insignificance. I had a shower then went to find the others in a bar down the road. I ordered a couple of beers, but then decided I should order four because I realised they were tiny, and they took so long to come. I drank them, and sat down to eat. I was ready for the sort of well deserved meal that you only really appreciate at the end of a hard day. Then the restaurant ran out of chips and I had to have salad instead. I can't remember being so disappointed with a meal. There was nothing wrong with it, it just wasn't the huge plate of steak and chips that I had been promising myself all day.

As the evening wore on, the chattiness of the group subsided as we all began to succumb to fatigue. I went to bed and instantly fell asleep.

Tomorrow I would be home, back to tell family and friends about it all and to watch the real professionals do it on the television.

Earlier in the day, I'd had a bit of extra support along the way in the shape of my Mum and Dad. They'd spent many rainy afternoons when I was a teenager driving me and Dicco to some desolate industrial estate to watch us race, but now they'd decided spend part of their holiday standing by a French roadside to watch me in my second Etape du Tour. They'd driven from where they were staying, had a night in a small rural hotel and driven at dawn to the top of the Col d'Izoard. I knew about where they'd be, but would have missed them if I hadn't heard my Mum shouting my name. I pulled over to the side of the road and after a big hug, had a drink and some of the home made flapjack that she'd thoughtfully brought with her. It was slightly surreal to stand there chatting to my parents and eating food from home. After a few minutes I said my goodbyes and set off down the other side of the mountain. Fortunately neither my Mum or Dad had looked at the road snaking its way down from their vantage point, otherwise I think mum would have tried to stop me, through fear of her eldest son putting himself in mortal danger.

What I didn't realize at the time was that home made flapjack wasn't the only thing mum and dad had done to help me on my way that day.

There has long been a tradition amongst fans of the Tour de France to paint names and slogans in the road. On my way along the route I had seen countless names of past heroes, political slogans, and many paintings of giant erect penises, often with a riders name attached. You can always see these on television coverage and I'm sure some of these 'artists' eagerly await the appearance of their own particular masterpiece on live television. When I got home, I went to a little cafe one afternoon and noticed that there was coverage of the Tour on a big television hanging from the wall. As I watched the bunch get to the top of the Col d'Izoard I could plainly see, on the road beneath their wheels, my own entry into the history of the tour, my own moment amongst the greats.

It said 'Allez Martin' across the road. My Mum and Dad had taken a tin of emulsion paint up a mountain and painted my name in huge letters and sitting there in a café Harrogate, I could see their handiwork on television. I wanted to tell the man behind the counter but was too emotional to speak. I hadn't even seen it as I rode over it but now I knew that for this year at least, my parents had made sure that I'd left my mark on the Tour de France. When I saw it I felt like another tiny bit of one of my wildest boyhood fantasies had come true.

Riding up Alpe d'Huez is certainly one of the things that would be on my list of 'One hundred things to do before you die'. I'm glad I did it, and I'm glad that I have done the Etape a few times. I'll probably do it a few more times too if I can stay fit enough. I might even try some other cycling challenges, after all, the Tour de France is only one part of the history of cycling. I'd like to sample a bit more of what makes it such a great sport. I don't care about the cheats – they'll always try to find a way to steal an advantage over their rivals, but it won't make a difference to me. I'll fall asleep after every long ride feeling content that I know how good it feels to ride a bike, how good it feels to go further and higher than I ever thought I would and no one can take that away from me or from anyone else who gets up early on a Sunday morning and leaves his or her family asleep while they enjoy the simple pleasure of riding a bike.

Even if I reach the point where I can't go in search of more and more challenges, I'm sure I'll keep on cycling – there are plenty more good times to be had, memories to form and friends to be made along the way.

Even though my dreams of climbing Alpine passes under a hot July sun didn't come true quite in the way I thought they would, I feel lucky, in some small way, that I know how it feels to struggle toward the sky, feeling every stroke of the pedals and every beat of my heart. I know the sensation of flying down mountainsides, down from above where the birds fly, with a smile on my face and the wind in my hair.